Inga Ettelt, Silvia Koch, Nicole Malik, Kevin Marc Patterson, Stefanie Phlippen, Anne Sutter

Herausgeberin: Sandra Deneke

navi Englisch 9/10

1. Auflage

Bestellnummer 61295

Bildungsverlag EINS

Diese Zeichen bei den Aufgaben sagen dir, was du tun könntest:

Track xx – Hört das Tonbeispiel an

Beschaffe dir Informationen

Schreibe in dein Heft

gr – Hier hilft dir die Grammatik-Seite weiter

Arbeit mit einem Partner oder einer Partnerin

Achtung! Hier musst du aufpassen

AH – Weitere Aufgaben im Arbeitsheft

P – Dieses Symbol kennzeichnet geeignete Aufgaben für das Portfolio

Diese Zeichen am unteren Rand sagen dir etwas zum Lernbereich:

Hören und Verstehen

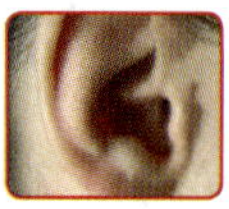

Sprechen

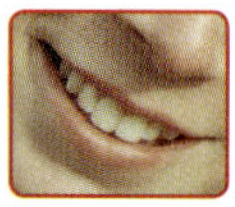

Schreiben

Mit Texten arbeiten

Wortschatz erweitern

Mit Sprache richtig umgehen

Hinweis: Die Nummerierung der Audio-Tracks basiert auf der Reihenfolge der Schülerbuchseiten und ihrer entsprechenden Arbeitsheftseiten.

Haben Sie Anregungen oder Kritikpunkte zu diesem Produkt?
Dann senden Sie eine E-Mail an 61295_001@bv-1.de
Autoren und Verlag freuen sich auf Ihre Rückmeldung.

www.bildungsverlag1.de

Bildungsverlag EINS GmbH
Sieglarer Straße 2, 53842 Troisdorf

ISBN 978-3-427-**61295**-7

Contents

1 At school:

Track 01

Modern communication

1 At school:

Back at school

Track 02

The summer holidays are over. Emily, Paul and the rest of their class are back at school. They've got a subject called ICT. But everyone says "We've got a computer lesson". In their first lesson the pupils can try out the computers. There are lots of things to do.

Paul writes an e-mail to his aunt Betty in America.

From: Paul94@freemail.uk
Sent: Thursday, 4/8/20.. 3:30 PM
To: BKeane@freemail.com
Subject: At school

Hi Aunt Betty,

I'm at school now and we're in our new computer room. It's brilliant: Everything is new and very modern – we've got the latest computer models that are very fast and we've got flat screens.
Our teacher Mr Perkins is really cool. He knows everything about computers.
The holidays were great. I hope Toby enjoyed his time in England. And I'm looking forward to going to America next year.
Bye for now and say hello to Uncle Bob.

Yours, Paul

AH

1. Read the text.
2. Find out all the computer words in the text. Make two lists in your exercise book. Write the words into the list. You can add more words:

computer hardware	things you can do with your computer

3. Talk about your own computer:
   - Have you got a computer?
   - What hardware have you got?
   - What do you do with the computer?

How to write an e-mail

Track 03

AH

Mr Perkins the ICT teacher wants to do an e-mail project with his class. Before he starts the project, he tells the class how to write an e-mail with a special e-mail program.

1

2
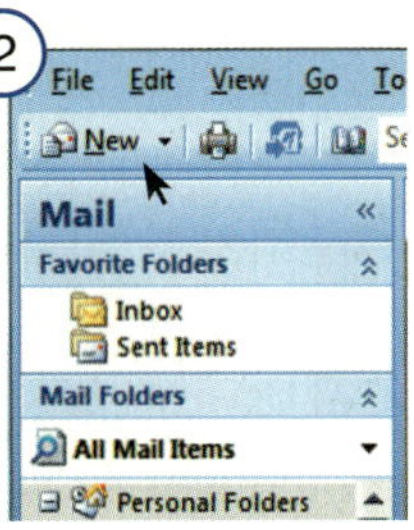

3
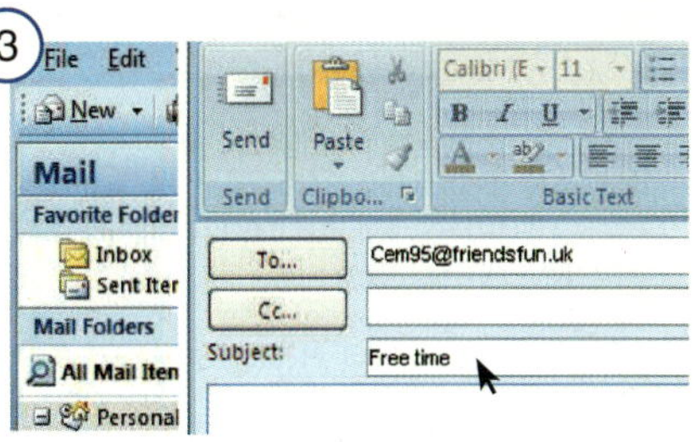

4
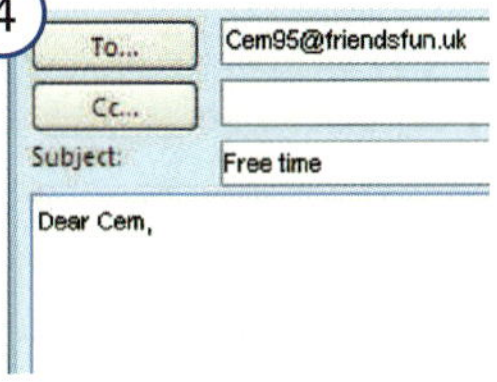

5
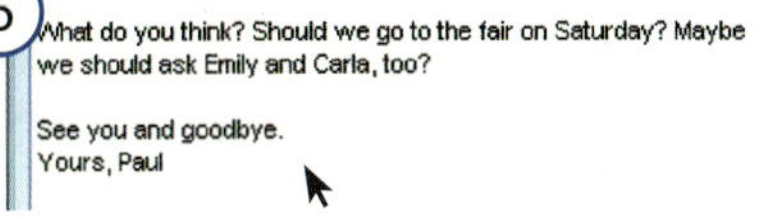

6

A. Write the text of your e-mail. Start with "Dear Cem".

F. Type in the e-mail address of your best friend and then write a subject into the "Subject"-field.

C. In the program choose the icon "New".

D. At the end of your e-mail tell your friend goodbye.

B. Click on the "Send"-button.

E. To start the program, you must double-click on the program icon.

1. Listen to Mr Perkins.
2. Match the texts and the pictures.
3. Tell your class how to write an e-mail.

eine E-Mail schreiben

1 At school:

E-pals

Track 04

Mr Perkins' ICT-class has started an e-mail project with pupils from all over the world. They write each other e-mails and talk about their countries, their families and their hobbies.

From: Amahle@freemail.za
Sent: Thursday, 4/23/20.. 10:44 AM
To: Emily95@freemail.uk
Subject: About me

Hi, my name is Amahle. I'm 14 years old and live in South Africa.
I don't like to talk about my family: my mother died when I was 8 years old.
I have two brothers and two sisters. I go to a boarding school. There I learn English. That's important because there are more than 10 different languages in South Africa. With my brothers and sisters I speak the Zulu language, but at school I must speak English. South Africa is a beautiful country with a lot of wild animals. You can see zebras and giraffes in the picture. The other picture is of me.
I like going to school because all my friends live in the school. I like playing handball. My friends and I often cook and dance together. That's nice. When I grow up I want to be a nurse. I like helping other people.

Sala Kahle – that's "goodbye" in the Zulu language – Amahle

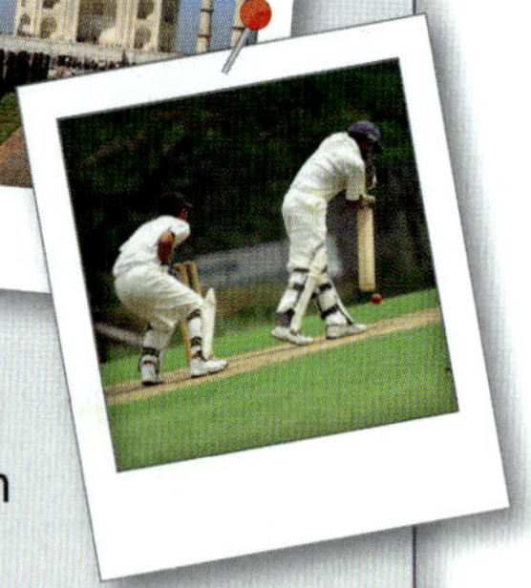

From: Samir@freemail.in
Sent: Thursday, 4/23/20.. 11:30 AM
To: Paul94@freemail.uk
Subject: About me

Hello, my name is Samir. I'm 15 years old. I live in Delhi, India with my family. We are six children in my family. My family has got the money to send us to school. But there are children in India who live on the streets. It's a big problem. India is a big country. Most people can speak English but at home we speak Hindi.
In my free time I like playing cricket and I like surfing the internet. Maybe we can chat with each other one day. I don't like writing letters but e-mails are OK. When I grow up I want to be a software programmer like my father. I send you two pictures. One is of the Taj Mahal. A prince built this palace as a mausoleum for his princess – it was a big love story. I can tell you about it in another e-mail. In the other picture you can see me.

Phir Milenge – that's "See you again" in Hindi – Samir

From: Matt@freemail.com
Sent: Thursday, 4/23/20 . . 10:30 AM
To: Cem94@freemail.uk
Subject: About me

Hi, my name is Matt. I'm from Montreal in Canada. I'm 15 years old. I live with my family: my mother, father and two older sisters in a nice house. In Montreal we don't speak English at home, we speak French. But most people in Canada speak French and English. In the picture you can see the skyline of Montreal. It's a big and beautiful city.
In my free time I like going fishing and camping with my father. I also like playing hockey but that's nothing special. I think every boy in Canada likes playing icehockey. The other picture shows me and my hockey team.
Hope to hear from your class soon.

Au revoir – that's "goodbye" in French – Matt

From: Andrea@freemail.de
Sent: Thursday, 4/23/20 . . 09:30 AM
To: Carla94@freemail.uk
Subject: About me

Hi there in England. Great to hear from you. I'm Andrea from Bremen in Germany. I'm 16 years old and I'm in year 9. I live in a flat with my mum and my younger brother.
I like listening to music and I like playing the guitar. I also like playing with my dog. But I don't like going for long walks with him. My mother says I must because he's my dog. We always fight about it. My brother never goes out with the dog. There's a picture of me and my dog at the beach of the Weser river. In the other picture you can see the "Bremen town musicians" – a famous story. Maybe I'll tell you about it in my next e-mail.

Tschüss – that's "goodbye" in German – Andrea

1. Read the e-mails.
2. Describe the pictures.
3. Choose one of the pupils. Make notes about him or her. Tell your partner about this boy or girl.
4. Can **you** write an e-mail to Paul's and Emily's class?
5. Which pictures would you send with your e-mail? Describe them.

AH

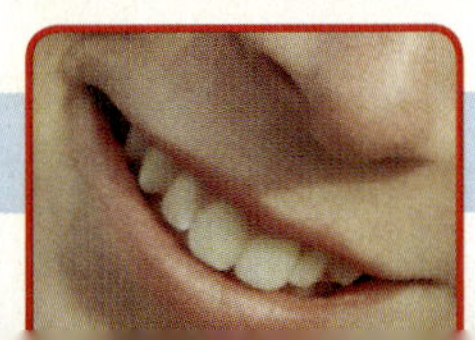

AH

Things we like and do not like doing

Matt

Samir

Andrea

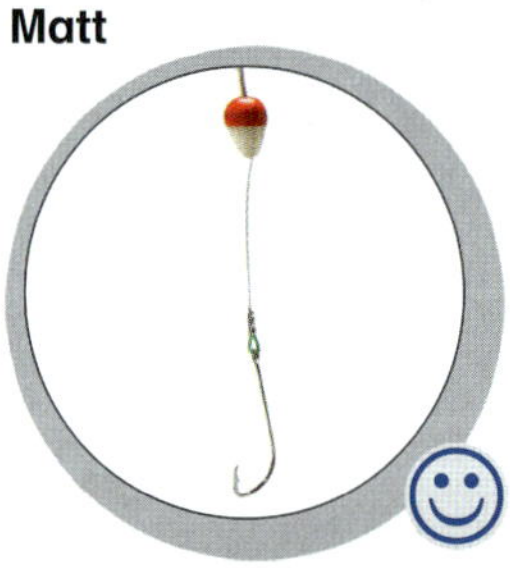

1. What do the boys and girls like doing?
2. What do the boys and girls not like doing?
3. And **you**? Tell the class.
   Say: *I like eating ice cream.*

4. Work with a partner. Ask him or her what they like.
   Ask: *Do you like surfing on the internet?*

I like **I don't like**	playing hockey reading books going for a walk in the park going to a restaurant dancing cooking surfing on the internet chatting with friends …	.
Do you like		**?**

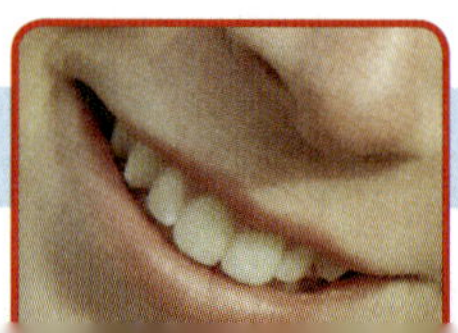

Strategy: Finding information on the internet

I must find more information about children in South Africa for Mr Perkins' class. I could go to the library, look into books or use the internet. On the internet I go to a search engine. Do you know these search engines?

This is what Paul does:	This is what you can do:
• Paul goes to www.google.co.uk. • Paul wants to know: "How do children in South Africa live?" • Paul's keywords are "children" and "South Africa". • Paul types in his keywords. • Paul quickly reads through the list of results. • Paul opens the page. • Paul finds some information. But he needs more, so he reads some of the other pages as well.	• Go to the search engine of your choice. • Think about a question that you want to ask. • Find two or three keywords in your question. Use verbs, adjectives or nouns as keywords only. • Type in the keywords and click on the "Search"-button. • Scan the results. That means you read through the short texts. Are they helpful? • Choose one or more pages and open them. • Does it contain the information you want? ☐ Yes? Great work. ☐ No? Check the other pages. Improve your search and think about other keywords.

1. You want to find out about the next concert of your favourite band.
   - What are your keywords?
   - Do the search. What can you find out?

Strategy: Be SMART

AH

www.kidsmart.org.uk

1. How do **you** use the internet?
   Say: *I often write e-mails.*

I	always often sometimes never	use the internet. write e-mails. chat with strangers. meet friends from the internet. tell my parents about what I do on the internet. tell strangers my phone number or address. …

P

2. Are **you** SMART?
   When is it important to remember the SMART rules?
   - Find one or more situations. Make notes.
   - Then tell your class about these situations.

This is what you have learned

S afe
M eeting
A ccepting
R eliable
T ell

A project

More about safe surfing

Do a project in class. Find out more about games, music, mobiles and social networks.

Each group chooses one topic and prepares a short presentation or makes a poster for the classroom wall.

Your research could start here:
http://www.kidsmart.org.uk/

A quiz

Use a search engine to answer these questions. Think of the keywords.

1. What is the capital of South Africa?
2. Which country is Bangalore in?
3. What language do the people speak in Quebec?
4. There are a lot of sights in Berlin. Name one.
5. There is lots of software to send e-mails with. Name one.
6. Explain the word "netiquette".

Now find more questions for your class.

2 Free time:

Track 05

Shopping

- a pedestrian zone
- to go shopping
- a shopping bag
- a café
- a shop
- a shop window
- a mobile phone
- an umbrella
- a cinema
- a price tag

Running late

Track 06

1

Carla, Emily and Paul want to go shopping together after school. They want to meet at four o'clock at the bus stop 'city centre'.

2

Carla and Paul are waiting for Emily at the bus stop. Paul looks at his watch: 4:15 p.m. Emily is 15 minutes late. Where is she? Did she forget about the shopping tour?

3

Carla tries to call Emily at home and on her mobile phone. No answer.

4

…

5

Now they can finally start their shopping tour.

AH

P

1. What happens in the 4th picture? Write it down and present it to your classmates.
2. Has anything like this ever happened to you before? Tell the class.
3. What do **you** think, how do Paul, Carla and Emily feel in this situation?
4. Choose one person and write a short internal monologue (an internal monologue is what people think without saying).

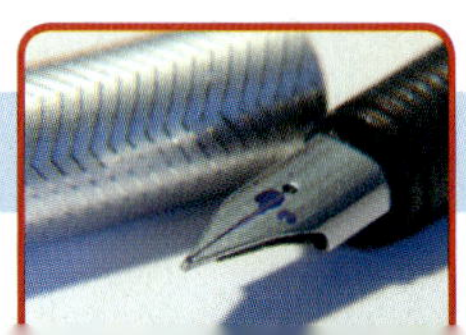

In the shop

Track 08

AH

Emily: "I need a new pullover. Can you help me find one?"

Paul: "Sorry, I want to have a look through down at the men's department. I'll catch up with you later. See you."

Emily and Carla: "See you later."

Carla: "I'll help you, Emily. Let's see. Oh, this one is very expensive."

Shop assistant: "Hello. How can I help you?"

Emily: "Hi. I'm looking for a pullover."

Shop assistant: "Alright then. What colour would you like?"

Emily: "I think a brown or a green pullover would be nice."

Shop assistant: "Do you prefer a special brand?"

Emily: "No, I don't care much about brands. They're more expensive."

Shop assistant: "Alright, here are some nice pullovers. What size do you wear?"

Emily: "I think a **M**edium."

Shop assistant: "How do you like this one?"

Emily: "It's nice, but **M**edium seems too large. I'll try a **S**mall one as well."

Shop assistant: "Here you are. What else can I do for you?"

Emily: "We are fine now. Thank you."

1. Listen to the dialogue.
2. Act the scene and show it to your class.

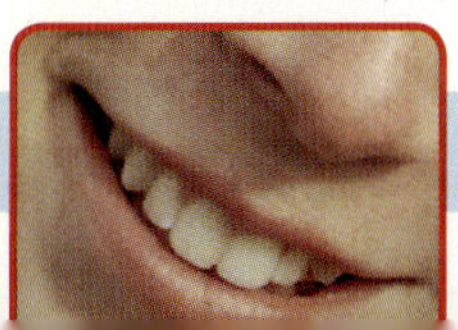

Decisions

Track 10

Emily: "Oh no, I can't decide which pullover I should choose."

Carla: "Choose the one you feel prettiest in. I think you look really pretty in the brown one."

Emily: "I think the green one is prettier. But it's the most expensive one. It costs £38.00. That's too much."

Paul: "I would choose the cheapest one. I think they all look very nice."

Emily: "Which one is the cheapest? The green one costs £38.00, the brown one £23.99 and the light brown one £25.00. Oh no, I don't want the pullover for £23.99. It's too dark."

Carla: "If this one is too dark and that one too expensive, then you made your decision. Take the pullover for £25.00. It's on sale and it was really expensive before."

Emily: "I think you're right. I'll take the light brown pullover for £25.00. What did you find, Paul?"

Paul: "Girls are so complicated. I found a pair of jeans, a cap and a T-shirt."

Emily: "We are not complicated. We just take our time to make the right decisions."

gr

AH

1. Listen to the dialogue.
2. Read the dialogue.
3. Act the scene.
4. How do **you** decide? Is there a difference between boys and girls making decisions? Discuss in class.

etwas abwägen

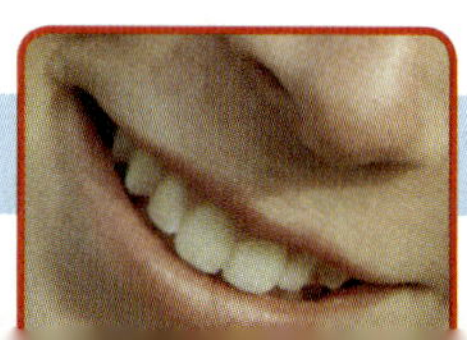

At a café

AH

1. Do **you** like going to a café?
2. What do people do in a café? What do people eat and drink in a café? Make a mind map.
3. What do people talk about in a café? Pick one of the tables and write a dialogue.

P

einen Dialog entwerfen

Where do you like to shop?

Track 14

There are many places to buy things:

in your hometown or in another city

on the internet

from a catalogue

on TV (teleshopping)

on the market

at your door

In former times shopping was different. People just went to the local market. Nowadays you have many options. You can go to stores in your hometown or the nearest city. But it's also really easy and fast to go to another city by train, by car or even by plane to shop there. You don't even have to leave your room because nowadays you can buy things via internet or you can order things out of a catalogue. You can even buy things on TV, which is called teleshopping. Besides these options there are people at your door, on the phone and in the street trying to sell things to you. And who knows what options we'll have in the future.

1. Read the text. If there is a word you don't know, look it up in your dictionary.
2. Where do **you** usually shop? What are the advantages and disadvantages of your type of shopping? Write a pro and contra list. Discuss it in class.
3. Ask a few people where they usually shop. Make a class survey.

Friday night

AH

1. What do **you** like to do on Friday/Saturday nights? Discuss in class.
2. What can **you** do in your town/nearest city? Make a mind map.

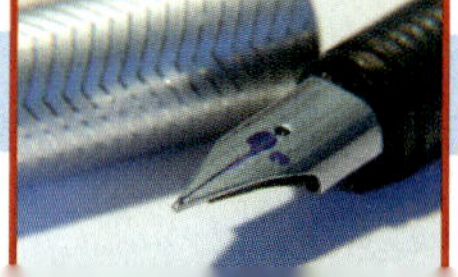

Strategy: How to make a chart

AH

Sometimes it's easier to look at a chart than to read or listen to a long explanation.
After you made your survey you can write down the answers in a chart.

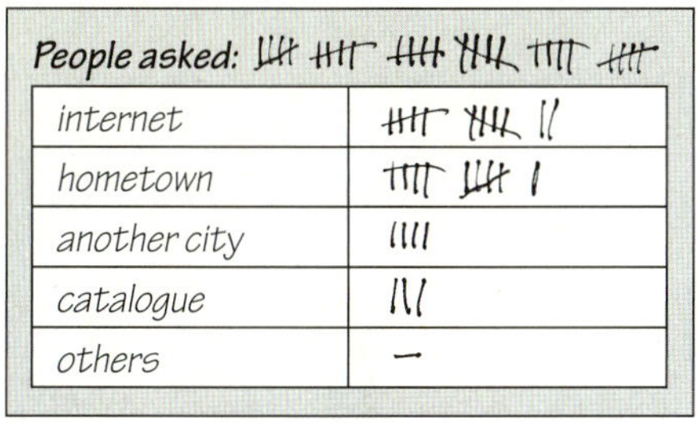

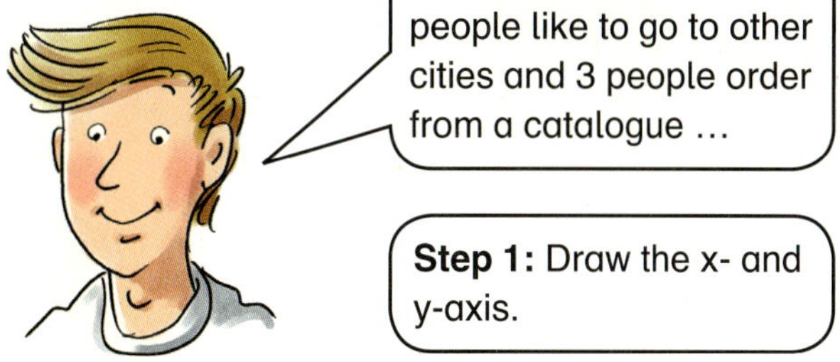

Step 1: Draw the x- and y-axis.

Step 2: Divide the y-axis.

Step 3: Put your results in the chart.

Step 4: Label your results.

Step 5: Write a headline and label the x- and the y-axis.

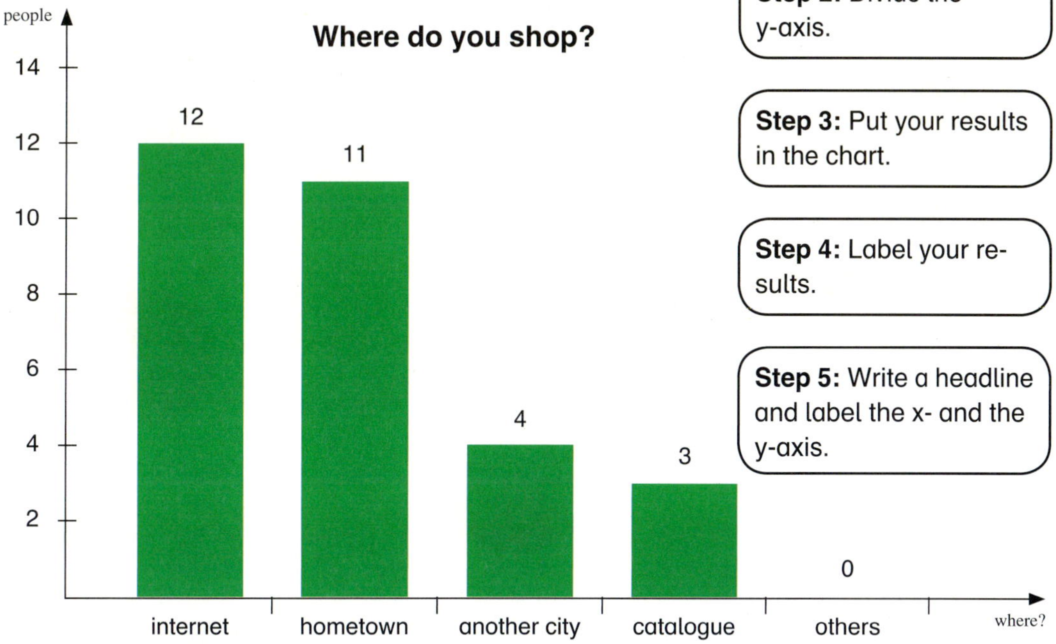

1. Make a chart in class. Use the results of your survey from page 23.
2. Think of a question with at least 3 different answers.
3. Ask all of your classmates and write down the answers.
4. Make a chart out of the answers. Present it to your class.
5. Do you know how to make charts with the computer? Try out different charts. Show them to your class.

P

This is what you have learned

START

You're late for a shopping trip. Why? Find a good excuse or go back to start.

Make a decision: Which T-shirt would you choose and why? Say: *I would choose …*

Or you have to skip one round.

You need to buy a T-shirt. To be faster, answer the shop assistant:

What are you looking for?
What colour do you like?
What size do you wear?
Do you like a special brand?

If you answered all the questions, roll the dice again.

What's the weather like?

Roll the dice:

1, 2 = sunny (play on normally)

3, 4 = rainy (skip one round and wait in a tearoom)

5, 6 = cloudy (maybe it will rain soon, hurry, roll the dice again)

Your best friend calls you and asks you what you're doing tonight. Answer your friend or go back 4 steps.

What's this? If you don't know, go 2 steps backward.

Nowadays there are different ways to buy things. You can go 1 step forward for every way you can name.

FINISH

Rules:

- You need: 1 dice, 1 token for each player.
- The youngest player starts.
- Put your token on start, throw the dice and move your token. If you get to a red field, follow the instructions. Answer in whole sentences.The winner is the player who reaches the finish field first.

3 About me:

Track 15

Love and friendship

- to flirt
- to date
- to get to know someone
- to have eye-contact
- to talk to each other
- to dream of someone
- to think of someone
- to stare at someone
- to have butterflies in the stomach
- to be attracted to someone
- to kiss someone
- to go out with someone

How to get to know people

Track 16

Real life situations

Mostly people get to know each other in real life situations such as on the streets or at school or during vacation.
These situations are “natural”. People get to know both: looks **and** character. If two people like each other they can meet again. The relationship develops slowly. One person can get to know the other person in different situations.

Speed dating

Speed dating is an organised matchmaking. Men and women sit in pairs in a room. After five minutes the organiser rings a bell. Each person takes notes on a piece of paper, then the men change places. The new pair starts to small talk for five minutes. Then the bell rings again and so on.
This way, each man and each woman have a short time to get to know each other. After the round each person hands the papers back to the organiser who does the matching. If both, man and woman, would like to meet again, the organiser gives them the addresses on the next day. Of course a person can only check the other person’s looks and interests. A person doesn’t get to know the other person’s character.

The blind date

On a blind date two people meet for the very first time. Sometimes they have not even communicated with each other before. So for both, man and woman, it is an absolute surprise whom they will get to see on a blind date. The match could be arranged by mutual friends or relatives.
Blind dates can be very disappointing: people have expectations. Blind dates – especially internet blind dates can be dangerous. It is very important to meet in public not in privacy.

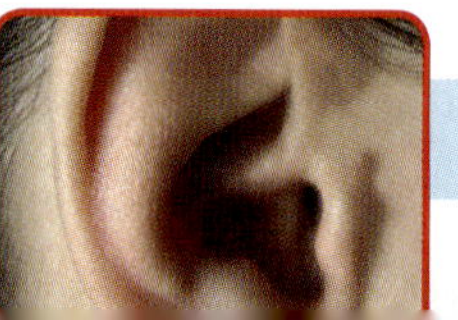

AH

1. Listen to the texts and read along.
2. Where else do people get to know each other? Collect in class.
3. Where do **you** get to know people?
   Where do **you** not get to know people?
   Talk about it with your neighbour. Say:

I **I don't**	get to know people	on the internet. in chat rooms. at school. at a club. at the shopping centre. during vacation. …

4. Look at the text about speed dating: What questions would **you** ask? Act a speed dating in class.

pros	cons
… it's anonymous.	… it's anonymous.
… it's exciting.	… it's dangerous.
… I'm shy.	… I'm too shy.
… I'm talkative.	… it's embarassing.
…	…

5. Make a list of pros & cons in class.

6. What about **you**? Talk about it with your neighbour.

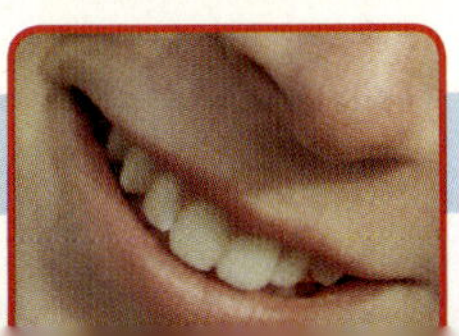

Pick-up lines

Track 17

AH

Lifestyle today

11

Before you get to know someone you have to make contact with the person. What could you do? What could you say? Eye-contact, mimic and gestures are important. But in many situations you will need a good pick-up line to start with.

Cool rules for hot dates

What do you know about dating? Here are some rules to make dating easier.

Dos!

- Brush your teeth.
- Be natural. Be yourself.
- Take a shower.

Donts!

- **Don't** eat garlic 24 hours before you're dating.
- **Don't** let your mom choose the clothes you wear on the date.
- **Don't** overdo the make-up.

gr

P

1. Read the two pick-up lines. What do **you** think? Do they work?
2. Think of good pick-up lines. Make a list. Talk about it in class.
3. Look at the dating rules. Can you add to the list of Dos! and Donts!? Collect in class.

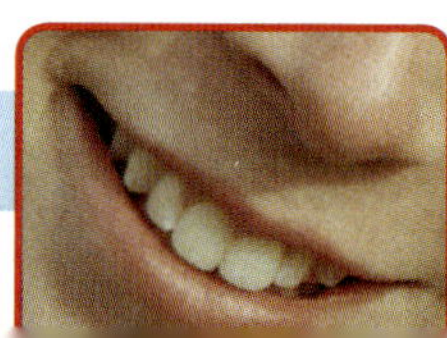

Matchmaking

Track 18

AH

Jacky and Jason work for the magazine “Lifestyle today”. Every month the magazine shows “the perfect pair”. Anybody can apply who is single. Each single sends an e-mail with a short text and a picture. Jacky and Jason discuss the e-mails, take notes and do the matchmaking. The “perfect pair” wins a prize: A candle-light-dinner at a fancy restaurant … and the chance to meet again.

Jacky: “OK, let’s find the perfect pair. Here are notes and pictures.”

Jason: “How about Lynne and Brian? They both like music.”

Jacky: “Yes, but he’s 35 years old and she’s 19. He’s much older than her. But also Lynne is tall. She’s taller than Brian.”

Jason: “That doesn’t really matter. But anyway, it’s not the perfect pair. Let’s look at Lynne and Tim. They’re both 19. She’s beautiful and he’s very handsome.”

Jacky: “Yes, but Tim dislikes pets. Lynne has three dogs.”

Jason: “Oh that’s true. Here … Janet and Tim. They’re both young. They both like playing basketball, meeting friends and cooking. And she looks as good as him. They’re perfect for each other.”

Jacky: “Great! They’re a perfect pair. They could be the winner of next month’s candle-light-dinner. Let’s look at the other singles.”

1. Listen to the dialogue and read along.
2. What are criteria for a perfect pair? What do **you** think? Discuss in class. Say:

gr

It’s **It’s not**	important that	she is as old as him. he is as sporty as her. he is taller than her. she is younger than him. …

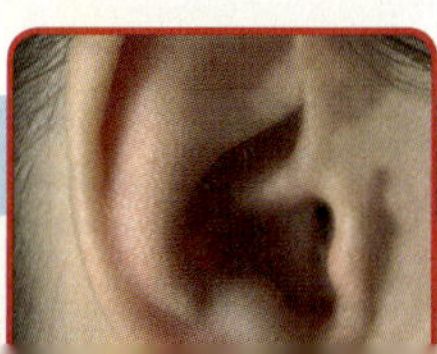

Love story I

Track 20

einen Dialog lesen und verstehen

AH

From: Emily95@freemail.uk
Sent: Thursday, 4/8/20.. 5:58 PM
To: perfectpartner@lifestyle-today.uk
Subject: Perfect partner

Hi, my name is Emily. I'm 15 years old and I live in Bristol. I'm 5 feet and 5 inches tall. I'm sporty. My hobbies are inline skating and playing volleyball. I like hanging out with my friends and going to the cinema. I love ice cream. I don't like moody people, they should stay at home. The boy of my dreams is tall, blond and has blue eyes. He should be as sporty as me and he should like to laugh.
Also he should like my best friend even though she's a bit crazy.
Thank you for looking for my perfect partner, cheers Emily. (10)

1. Listen to the dialogue and read along.
2. Design a website for the magazine "Lifestyle today". Use the title "Find your pefect partner"!

P

AH

Love story II

From: perfectpartner@lifestyle-today.uk
Sent: Monday, 4/12/20.. 5:23 PM
To: Emily95@freemail.uk
Subject: Re: Perfect partner

Lifestyle today

Dear Emily, Congratulations!
You are the winner of the candle-light-dinner. We found the perfect partner for you.
He is waiting for you this Friday at 7 p.m. in the restaurant SPACE DINER. Be there!

❤❤❤

Kind regards,
Jacky & Jason

Lifestyle today
– editorial office –
New Way, Avonmouth
Bristol BS11 9DJ

1. Look at the story. What do you think – what will happen with Emily and Paul?

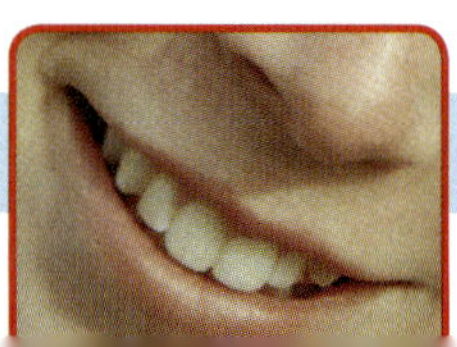

Favourites

Track 21

What should the girl of your dreams be and look like?

My name is Scott.
The girl of my dreams should have brown eyes and long black curly hair. She should have a lovely figure and beautiful lips with shiny white teeth. She should have a big smile. The girl of my dreams should be shy with others but not with me. We talk a lot with each other. She should listen to my problems and she should be a real friend. The girl of my dreams should be romantic.

What should the boy of your dreams be and look like?

My name is Lara.
The boy of my dreams should be tall and blond. He should have got green eyes and long eyelashes. The boy of my dreams should be friendly and respectful with others. The boy of my dreams should be sporty and entertaining. But my boyfriend has dark hair and brown eyes and he's as tall as I am. He hates sports and prefers computer games. He has the friendliest face in the world though … and I love him.

1. Talk about the girl/boy of your dreams in class. What is important to you?
   Say: *The smile is important to me.*
   The eyes are important to me.

AH

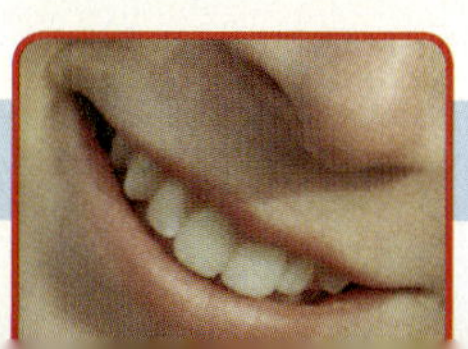

3 About me:

Strategy: Taking notes

Track 22

Taking notes helps to focus on the important facts. You can take notes from out of a text:

1. Mark the keywords.

From: Owen.Be@freemail.uk
Sent: Wednesday, 4/7/20.. 8:12 PM
To: perfectpartner@lifestyle-today.uk
Subject: About me

Hi, my name is Owen. I'm 16 years old. I have short dark hair and brown eyes. I'm 5 feet and 10 inches tall. My look is casual: I like to wear jeans and shirts. I go to school in London. I like meeting friends. I hang out and laugh a lot with them. We often do sports together. I dislike aggressive people. I've had bad experiences with that. My hobbies are playing football and judo. I do lots of sports. I think it's important that you can rely on people. So I'm looking for a girl I can count on, who likes to meet people and who has a good sense of humour.

2. Take notes like the following. Use bullet points (•), start with small letters and don't use punctuation.

Owen

- 16
- sporty
- 5 feet and 10 inches
- likes playing football

3. You can also take notes to organise your own ideas. Sometimes it helps to organise them in a table.

name	age	looks	likes
Owen	16	sporty	Football, judo

AH

P

1. Take notes. Use the text in your workbook.
2. Write a profile. Use portraits from magazines. Present it to the class.
3. Organise a matchmaking in class.

This is what you have learned

Play with a partner. You are person number 1. Your partner is person number 2. Act the dialogues.

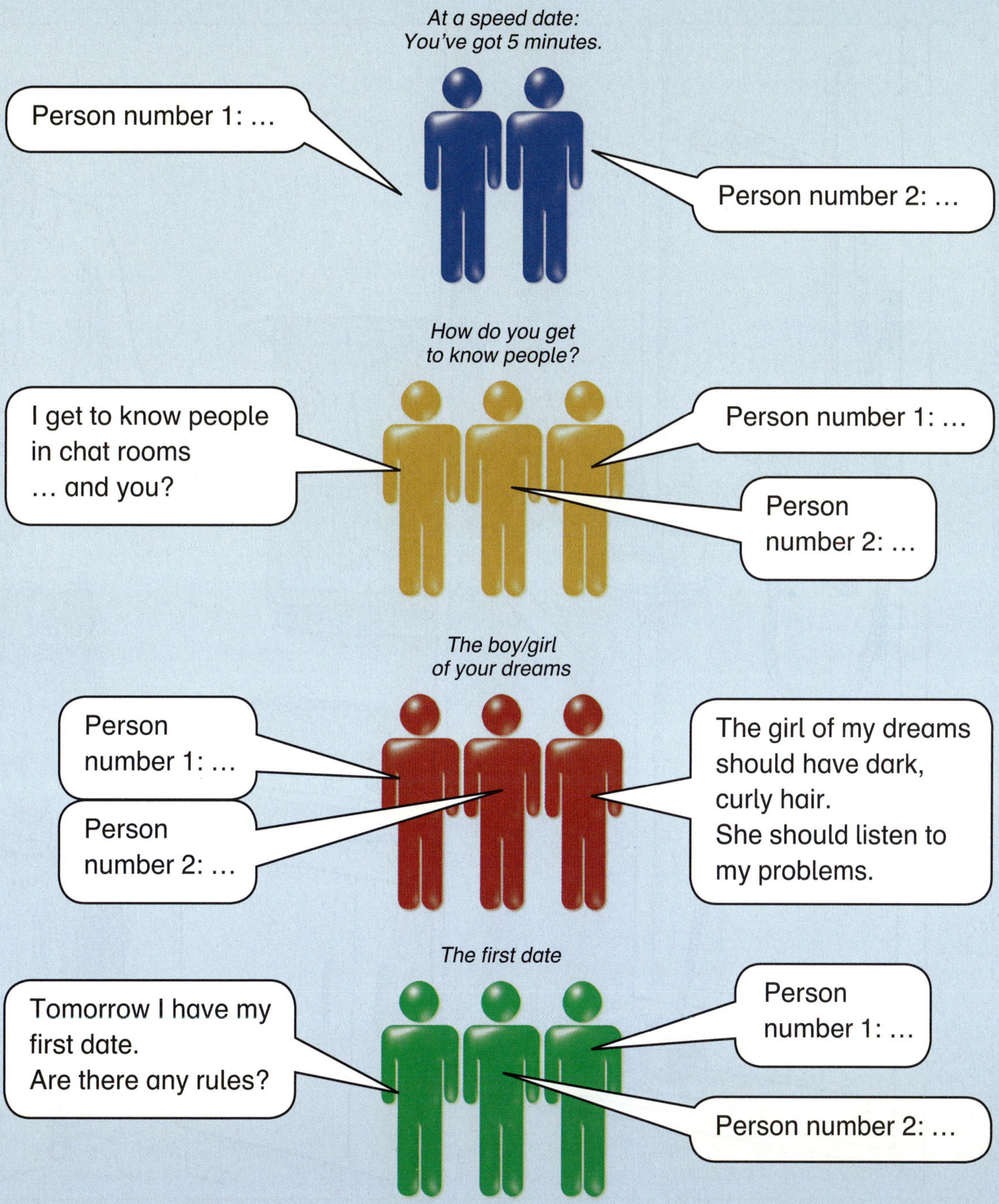

4 My body:

Track 24

Lifestyle and fashion

Paul and Emily get ready for their date

Track 25

Emily: "Should I wear a skirt or trousers?"

Carla: "Wear a skirt and put on your black tights. That looks great on you."

Emily: "Should I wear the blouse or the top?"

Carla: "Come on, you're going to the cinema, not to the opera. Take the top."

Emily: "I'm ready."

Carla: "Let's see … there are some accessories missing. I brought some of my jewellery with me. Earrings make outfits look much better. Belts are also very fashionable nowadays. Put on my belt."

Carla: "I remember your yellow hair circlet. Where is it?"

Emily: "Just a second. I'll take it."

Carla: "Also put on your new shoes and take your favourite handbag. Wow, Paul will be impressed."

Emily: "Thanks Carla, what would I do without you!?"

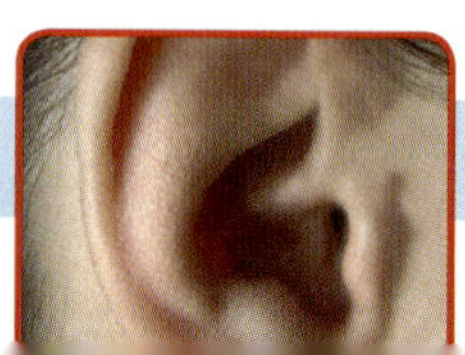

Cem: "Paul, are you there?"

Paul: "I'm in the bathroom. I'm a bit late. I just had a shower and have to shave now. Make yourself at home. What do you think about my outfit?"

Cem: "Well... checked and striped is a no-go."

Paul: "Really? OK, I'll put on my jeans."

Cem: "Much better. But your hair ... can you get me your hair gel? I'll make you a cool hairstyle."

Paul: "Just a second. Remember Cem, I have a date with EMILY. My hair has to look perfect."

Cem: "I know. Trust me... Finished! You have to hurry up now. Dating rule number one: don't be late! "

Paul: "Thanks for helping me, Cem. I owe you."

1. Listen to the CD and read along.
2. What would **you** wear for a date?
   Say: *I would wear ...*

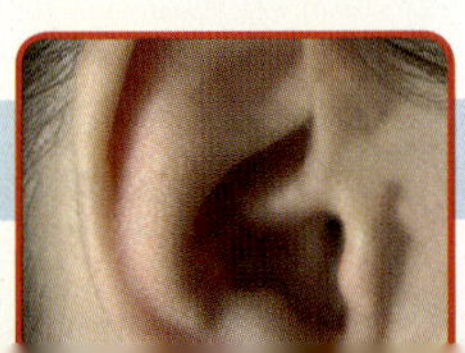

Fashion in former times

Track 26

AH

Fashion in the 50s

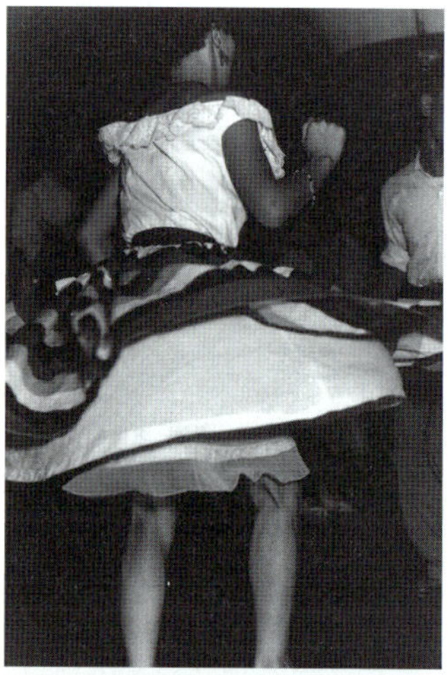

In the 50s it was important for women to accentuate the hips with bodice. At that time women wore skirts called petticoats and pencil skirts.

Accessories like hats, handbags and gloves in the same colour as the clothes were a must. Hats were also a must for men. Men wore the business look.

Women in the 50s had curly hair. Straight hair was out. Short hair was in. Many women and men had a hair cut called "Bob".

Fashion in the 60s

This time was also called "The wild 60s". The miniskirt with the new developed tights was a must for young people in the 60s. For men it was in to wear pullovers over shirts. The 60s were also famous for the hippie look: flared trousers and batik fabrics. Accessories were less important during the 60s.

Fashion in the 70s

Clothes with a floral design and flared trousers were very fashionable at that time. Men and women wore platform shoes. Big accessories were in. Big sunglasses and belts were a must. Men and women had long hair in the 70s. Men had chops.

Fashion in the 80s

The colour of the clothes in the 80s was often neon. Carrot pants, leggings, legwarmers, wide pullovers and shoulder pads were popular. Brooches and long necklaces were a must. Headbands were also very trendy. The blow-dry hairstyle and the permanent wave was famous in the 80s. Men used hair gel.

Fashion in the 90s

Fur patterns were common for clothes. Platform shoes had a revival in the 90s. Baggy pants and flannel shirts were also popular. Men had erect hair with blond hair-ends. Women had single coloured strands of hair. Piercings und tattoos were popular accessories in the 90s.

Fashion today

?

1. Look at the pictures. What is typical for each period?
2. What is fashionable today?
3. Listen to the CD and read along.
4. Look up words you do not know in the dictionary.
5. Ask your parents, relatives or other friends older than 40 years for pictures when they were young. Bring them along and discuss.

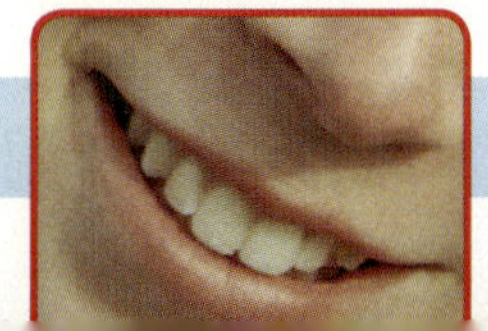

AH

What's your opinion?

A

B

C

D

E

F

1. Which outfit do you like the most? Explain.
   Say: *I like outfit A because …*

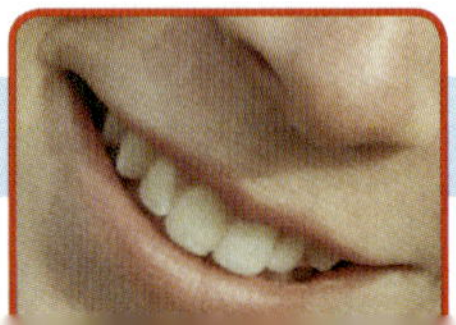

How to fold clothes

Track 27

AH

1. Put down the pullover.

2. Fold one side of the pullover half way down so that the fold ends with the collar.

3. Fold down the sleeve at the line shown in the picture.

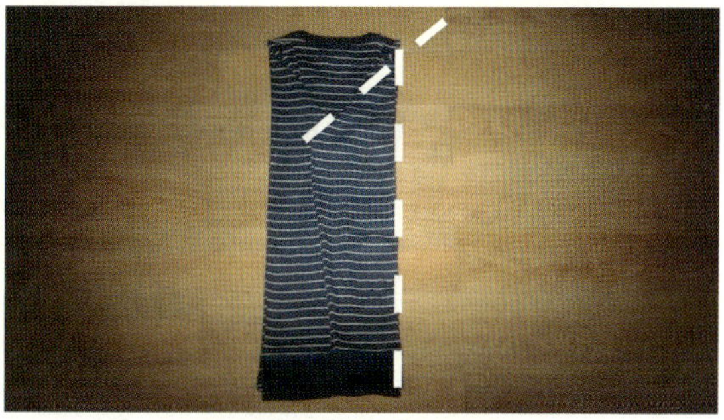

4. Repeat steps 2 and 3 with the other side of the pullover.

5. Fold the bottom half up to the collar.

6. Turn over the pullover. You've finished.

1. Do **you** fold clothes? Make a survey.
2. Listen to the CD and read along.
3. Take pullovers and try to fold them as shown above.

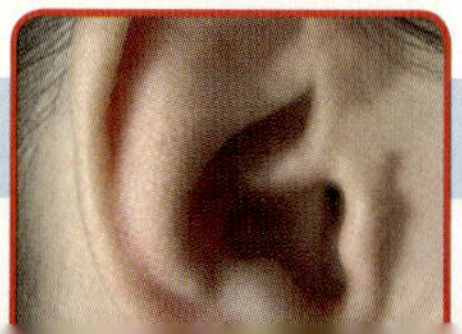

Strategy: Dictionary work

AH

By using multilingual dictionaries,

... you can translate from and into different languages.
... you can look up the meaning of words in foreign languages.
... you can look up words to spell them correctly.
... you can look up words to pronounce them correctly.

Note: Some words <u>cannot</u> be looked up directly

- Paul **has** a date with Emily. (3rd person singular ➔ have)
- Carla and Emily love **shoes**. (plural ➔ shoe)
- Emily **bought** a new handbag. (irregular verb ➔ buy)

1. Take a dictionary and look up the abbreviations used in the dictionary.

This is what you have learned

Create your own lifestyle magazine:

- Look for pictures in magazines or make own photos. Write short sentences about the pictures or photos.
- Write how to make fashionable clothes, accessories and hairstyles on your own. Make photos for a better understanding.
- Write texts about fashion:
  - What are famous people wearing?
  - What is in and what is out?
  - What was worn in former times?
  - Write about make-up. Take photos if possible.
- Create a cover.
- Write a table of content.

5 The world of work:

Track 29

AH

Experiencing work

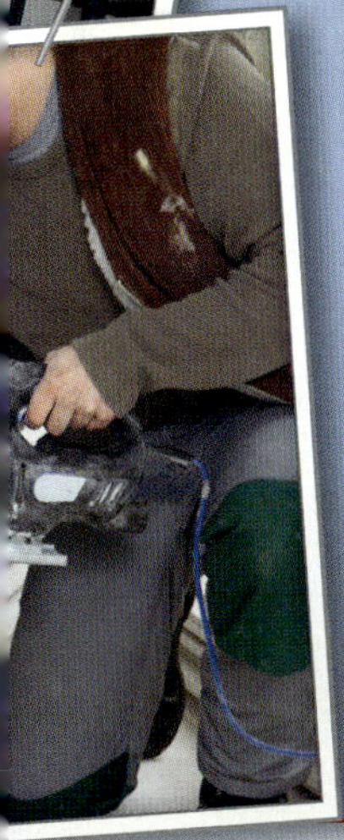

- a nurse
- a firefighter
- a hairdresser
- a factory worker
- a cook
- a cashier
- a mechanic
- a shop assistant
- a baker
- a painter and decorator
- a craftsman/ a craftswoman
- a nursery teacher

5 The world of work:

Looking for a work experience

Track 30

AH

Paul and Cem have to look for a work experience. After a football match they relax in the park and discuss their options.

Paul: "Where do you do your work experience, Cem?"

Cem: "I have an uncle, he works in a bakery. I can do it there."

Paul: "Goodness, you have to get up early!"

Cem: "I know – we start at 5 o'clock every morning. But I'm off at 1 p.m. already and that's cool. And you?"

Paul: "I have no idea. What could I do?"

Cem: "What interests you? Would you like to work in an office?"

Paul: "No, I think that's boring."

Cem: "Would you like to work in a factory?"

Paul: "Hhmm … I think that's hard work, isn't it?"

Cem: "It's just a work experience, it's not forever. Would you like to work in service?"

Paul: "As a waiter or a shop assistant? No, I think that's stressful. I would like to work as a craftsman."

Cem: "Well, that sounds like a plan. You could apply for a work experience as a plumber or a roofer or a bricklayer …"

Paul: "… or a painter and decorator. Yes, that's it! I'll ask at a painter's. Let's check the yellow pages for addresses."

1. Listen to the text.
2. Talk about the text:
   - What do Paul and Cem talk about?
   - Where does Cem do his work experience? What are his working hours?
   - What are Cem's ideas for Paul? What are Paul's ideas?

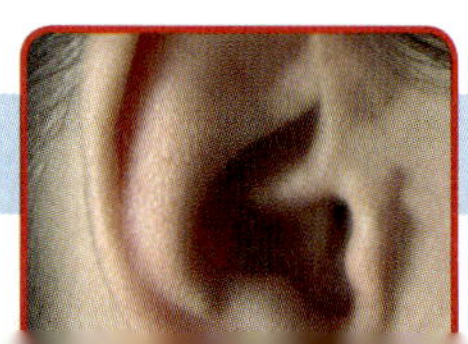

A Curriculum Vitae

I need your Curriculum Vitae.

Curriculum Vitae

name: Paul Morris

address: Ocean Drive, Bristol

telephone number: 0117-24682940

age: 16

nationality: British

school: Rosa Parks School

favourite subjects: music, sports, IT

work experiences: delivering newspapers, helping my father in his garage

activities/hobbies: listening to music, playing basketball and football, meeting friends, playing computer games

foreign languages: Spanish (basics)

skills: computer programs: Word, PowerPoint

6/14/20.. Paul Morris

1. Read the Curriculum Vitae.
2. Write your own Curriculum Vitae.
3. Where would you apply?
   Say: *I would apply at a/an …*

P

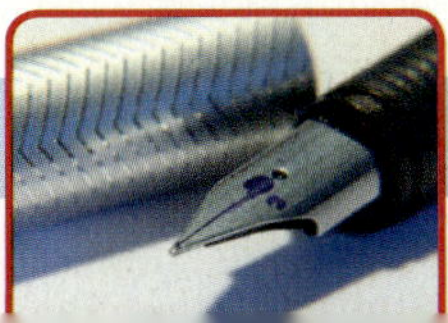

What would they like to be?

Claudia

Monica

Chris

Scott

Lisa

Darren

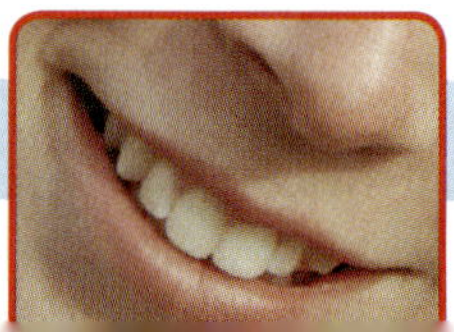

Reasons

… because	I like to work outside/inside. the job is easy/ great/interesting. the job makes good money. I like the working hours/working clothes. I'm good at it. I like to work with my hands. I like to cook/to drive/to travel/to help others. I like children/animals/flowers/cars. …

1. Listen to the teenagers on CD. What would they like to be?
   Say: *Lisa would like to be a/an …*
2. What would **you** like to be?
   Say: *I would like to be a/an …*
3. Listen to the teenagers again. What are their reasons?
   Say: *Lisa would like to be a cook because she likes to cook.*
4. Read the reasons. Think of other reasons in class.
5. What would **you** like to be? Give a reason.
   Say: *I would like to be a craftsman because I like to work with my hands.*

Track 31

Track 32

AH

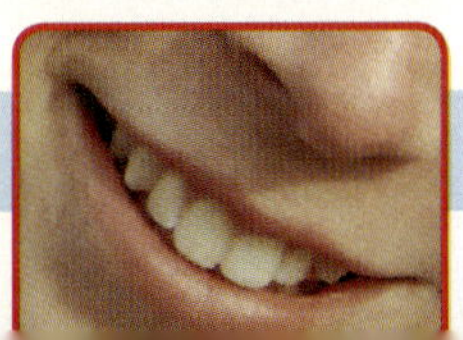

5 The world of work:

A profile

Track 34

AH

job: mechanic

name: Robert Moffit

age: 26

working hours: 7 a.m. – 4 p.m.

working clothes: comfortable, old sweatshirt, boots, blue working trousers, helmet

working place: at the harbour

colleagues: many colleagues

likes/dislikes: the harbour/doesn't like sitting around

family situation: wife (Jessica) and son (Mat)

hobbies: listening to music (German Hip Hop)

This is Robert. He is 26 years old. He is a mechanic and works at the harbour. His working hours are from 7 a.m. to 4 p.m. He wears working boots and blue working trousers. He also wears comfortable and old sweatshirts that can get dirty. He always wears a helmet at work for protection. Robert likes his job. He doesn't like sitting around. He likes working with his hands and he loves the harbour. He has many colleagues. His best buddy is Steven. Robert has a wife, Jessica, and a two-year-old son. His name is Mat. Robert's hobby is music. He loves German Hip Hop.

P

1. Read the notes.
2. Listen to the text on CD. Read the text.
3. Compare the text with the notes.
4. Choose a portrait picture from a magazine.
   Take notes and write a work profile.

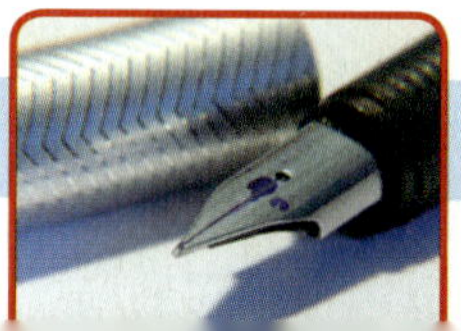

Job profiles

Track 36

at a bar

in a salon

at a bakery

at a supermarket

at people's home

at a garage

AH

1. Look at the pictures.
   What are these people's jobs? Where do these people work?
   Say: *Linda is a baker. She works at a bakery.*
   Sam is a … . *He works … .*
2. Write the sentences into your exercise book.
3. Listen to the text on CD. Who is speaking?

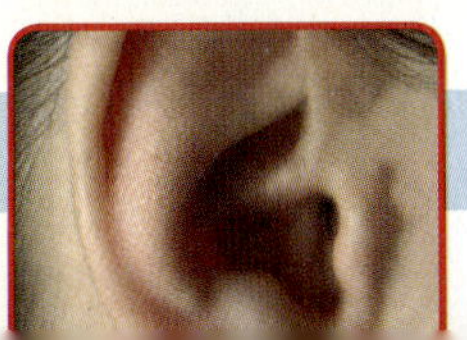

Job advertisements

Track 37

1

Paperboys and Papergirls

We are looking for newspaper boys and girls in the area around Bristol.

- Are you between 14 and 20 years old?
- Do you have a bike?
- Are you always punctual?
- Are you reliable?
- Do you have time on Mondays and on Thursdays?

Then we are looking for YOU!
Please apply to
Ms Jackson, Purple Paper,
15 Main Street, Bristol

2

Shop assistants for supermarket

We are looking for reliable people for our supermarket in this area.

Applicants should be between 16 and 50 years old. They should have some work experience.

We offer a good salary.

Please apply to
Mr Nelson, Nelson's Superstore
20 Hill Road, Bristol

3

Waiter or waitress for new café

We are looking for a waiter or a waitress for our new café.

Are you between 16 and 25?
Are you polite and quick?
Are you flexible with working hours?

Then apply to
Mrs Striker, Mellow Moon Café,
202 Madison Road, Bristol

4

Models wanted

We are looking for models:

- males and females
- age: 14 – 18
- with an interesting look
- no model experiences necessary

Applications to
Ms Sunshine, ProCast Studio
71 Walton Drive, Bristol

Track 38

AH

P

1. Listen to the CD. Read the ads.
2. Listen to the job interviews on CD. Which job does Emily apply for? Which job does Paul apply for?
3. Choose one of the jobs. Apply for the job.
4. Act an interview in class.
5. Create your own ad. Work with a partner.

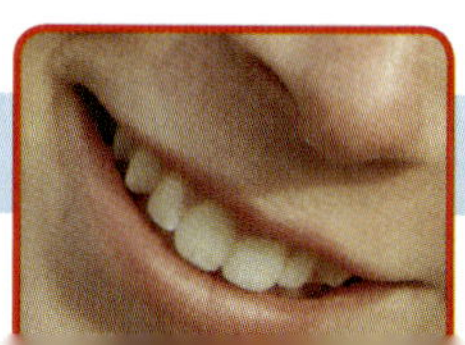

Strategy: From notes to text

From notes ...	... to text
job: painter and decorator	Painter and Decorator
working place: flats, offices	Painters work in flats or offices.
working hours: 7 a.m. – 4 p.m.	Painters work from 7 in the morning until 4 in the afternoon.
working clothes: overall	They wear an overall, so that the clothes don't get dirty.
salary: about £300 per week	They get about £300 per week.
pros: productive – you can see the results	Working as a painter is very productive and you can see the great results.
cons: hard work, unhealthy	But it is hard work and the paint is unhealthy.

1. Choose a job. Find information (internet, interview).
2. Write a work profile and present it to the class.

P

This is what you have learned

Play with a partner.
You need a coin and two tokens.
Flip the coin. Head = 1 field,
Number = 2 fields.
There are three different types of tasks. Write down the points.

RED Name the vocabulary.
➔ 1 point

BLUE Answer the question.
➔ 2 points

GREEN Act the dialogue with your partner.
➔ 3 points for you and 3 points for your partner.

START

Apply for the job.

What would you like to be?

What would you like to be? Give a reason.

What kind of information do you give in a Curriculum Vitae? Name 5 issues.

Apply for the job.

FINISH

6 At home:

Track 39

Family matters

- a dad
- a mum
- parents
- a son
- a daughter
- a grandmother
- a grandfather
- a grandchild
- a family
- a telephone
- a talk
- a television
- a mobile phone
- a school report

6 At home:

Track 40

AH

Talking in the schoolyard

Paul and Emily are in the schoolyard. Their friend Tom is with them. The three are talking with each other.

Paul: “Hey Tom, what’s wrong? You look sad.”
Tom: “I do not only look sad, I feel sad.”
Emily: “Why? What’s wrong?”
Tom: “It’s my parents. They want to divorce.”
Paul: “Oh, I’m sorry to hear that. Why do they want to divorce?”
Tom: “They argue and shout all the time. It’s no good anymore, they say.”
Paul and Emily: “How can we help you?”
Tom: “I’m sorry. I don’t really know.”

1. Before you read the text: Describe the picture.
2. Why is Tom sad?
   Say: *Tom is sad because …*
3. What can Paul and Emily do to help Tom?
   Say: *Paul and Emily can …*

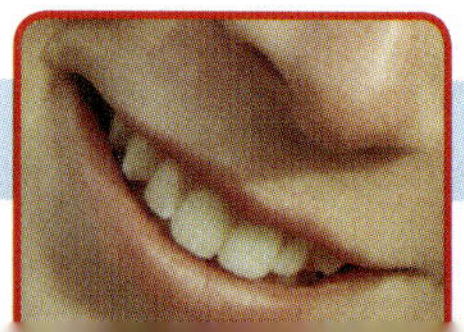

What can friends do?

Track 41

Paul and Emily are at Paul's house together with his parents. They talk about what Tom told them.

Dad: "Hey you two. What's going on?"

Paul: „Mum, Dad, we don't know what to do. Can we ask for advice?"

Mum: "Sure. Go ahead."

Emily: "It's Tom. His parents want to divorce. We would like to help him but we don't know how."

Paul: "Have you got any ideas? I'm sure many things will change for Tom."

Dad: "Why don't you take him out to the cinema?"

Paul: "Do you think that helps?"

Mum: "I don't think so. Talk to him. Give him the feeling he's not alone."

Emily: "Yes, I think that's a good idea. We'll watch a film at the cinema first and then we'll talk with him."

1. Read the text. Which advice do Paul's parents give?
2. What would **you** do?
   Say for example: *I would go to the cinema.*

6 At home:

Roles in a family: Yesterday and today

Track 42

AH

Paul and Emily are still thinking about what Paul's parents said. Now they're looking at a photo album. Some photos show Paul's parents, some show him on his own or with his parents.

Dad: "Hey, do you remember this, Paul?"

Paul: "Yes, I do. That was nice."

Mum: "Families in the past did a lot together, compared to today."

Emily: "Yes, I think so, too. In the past, the roles between husband and wife were different. Many women didn't work in a company, for example. They had enough to do at home. Cleaning, looking after the children and so on."

Paul: "And the husband used to go to work."

Dad: "Today, things are different. Husband and wife share the work. Roles are not as stiff as they used to be. A man can do as much housework as a woman. There's no difference."

Mum: "And women can earn as much money as men."

1. Read the text. Try to summarise.
2. What do **you** think of families of yesterday and of today:
   What has changed? What is still the same?
   Say: *In the past, …*
   Today, …
   Example: *In the past women worked at home.*

3. Do you agree with what they say?

The patchwork project

Track 43

In art, the word "patchwork" describes a special style, in which you can mix and arrange objects or pictures in any way you like.
Today it's also a word that is used to describe particular family constellations. It can mean that separated parents have new partners. That can mean that two half families are combined in one new family.

1. Read the text.
2. Try to find an explanation for the word "patchwork". What does the word "to patch" mean?

3. Collect magazines and newspapers. Design your own patchwork project about families. Make a picture or a painting or a collage.

P

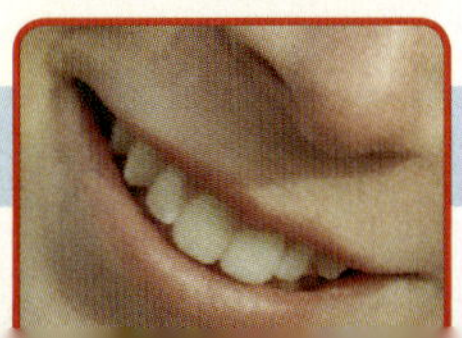

A walk in the park

Track 44

AH

Paul and Emily are in the park with Tom. They're sitting on a bench. Tom has some photos with him which he wants to show to Emily and Paul.

Tom: "Hey, this is us in the zoo."

Paul: "It looks like you had fun. Who is that with you?"

Tom: "That's my uncle. He's nice. You can have a lot of fun with him."

Emily: "And who is the lady?"

Tom: "That's my aunt. My uncle couldn't live without her."

Emily: "What about your parents, Tom? Did they talk with you about separating?"

Tom: "No. I just know that Dad says he doesn't want to live with Mum anymore. And she says she would give him another chance. I honestly don't know what to think of them."

Paul: "Well, at least there's a chance for them."

Tom: "It just wouldn't be the same without them."

Paul: "We'll keep our fingers crossed. But they're still your parents. That will never change."

Tom: "Thanks, Paul. Thanks, Emily."

1. Read the text. What is it about?
   Say: *The text is about …*
2. Act the scene.

A musical digression: "Family Portrait"

Track 45

This is a photo of P!NK.

Momma please stop cryin', I can't stand the sound
Your pain is painful and it's tearin' me down
I hear glasses breakin' as I sit up in my bed
I told dad you didn't mean those nasty things you said

You fight about money, 'bout me and my brother
And this I come home to, this is my shelter
It ain't easy growin' up in World War III
Never knowin' what love could be, you'll see
I don't want love to destroy me like it has done my family

Can we work it out? (Can we?) can we be a family? (Can we?)
I promise I'll be better (I promise), mommy I'll do anything (I'll do anything)
Can we work it out? Can we be a family?
I promise I'll be better, daddy please don't leave

Daddy please stop yellin' (Stop), I can't stand the sound (Can't stand the sound)
Make mama stop cryin', 'cause I need you around (yeah)
My mama she loves you (I know it), no matter what she says it's true
I know that she hurts you, but remember I love you, too

I ran away today, ran from the noise, ran away (Ran away)
Don't wanna go back to that place, but don't have no choice, no way
It ain't easy growin' up in World War III
Never knowin' what love could be, well I've seen
I don't want love to destroy me like it did my family

[...]

1. Listen to the song.
2. Read the lyrics of the song.
3. Can you say what the song is about? Make short notes.
   Say: *The song is about...*
4. Project: What is your favourite song? Work on a report about the song and/or the musician who wrote it.

P

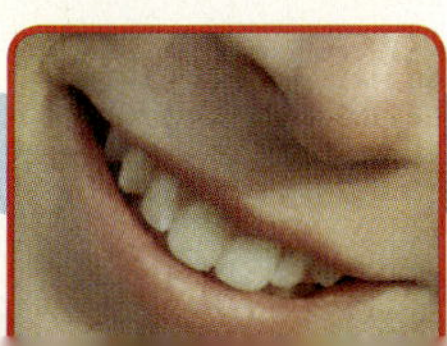

Strategy: Making diagrams

AH

A family tree shows you how you're related to the members of your family.

Can you draw your own family tree?

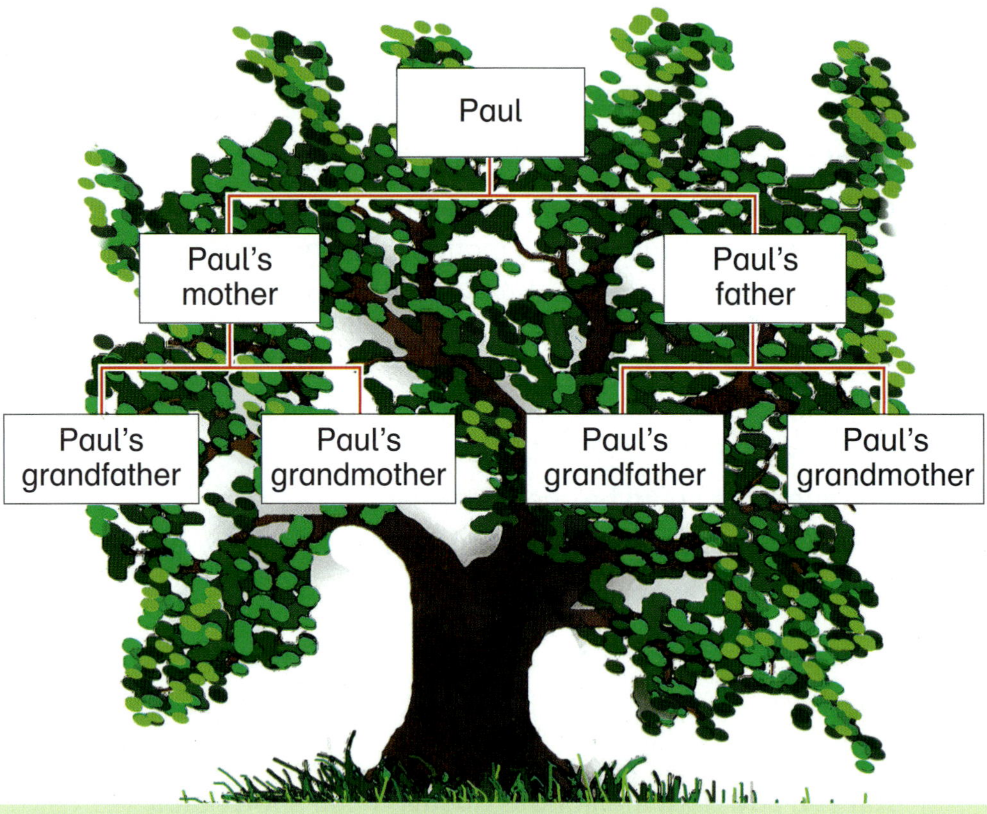

P

1. Draw your own family tree on an A3-sheet of paper.
   Put in your grandparents, your parents and yourself.
2. Can you put more members of your family into the tree?

This is what you have learned

Bingo

- Each pupil has one sheet of paper with family words on it.
- There are different versions of this sheet of paper.
- One person reads out the words one by one.
- The pupils cross out the words that they have.
- The pupil who is first to cross out three in a row wins the game.

Enjoy yourselves.

7 Around town:

Track 47

What if ...

- *the Citizens Registration Office*
- *the City Hall*
- *a police station*
- *a hospital*
- *a library*
- *a big building*
- *a small building*
- *a column*
- *a bus station*
- *a taxi stand*

7 Around town:

Track 48

Meeting friends

Paul and some of his friends meet in the park. They want to spend some time with each other, but they don't know what to do.

Paul: "It's such a nice day. But what can we do?"
Cem: "We could go and play football."
Emily: "Or we could see a film at the cinema."
Carla: "Or we could go shopping."
Paul: "What if we just stay here in the park and relax?"
Cem: "How boring. There's plenty of time to sit around and relax later."
Paul: "That's true. Let's go and have an ice cream."
Emily: "That's a good idea. Let's do that. There's a new ice-cream parlour near the Citizens Registration Office."

1. Read the dialogue between the friends.
2. What is the dialogue about? What would **you** like to do?
   Say: *I would like to stay in the park.*

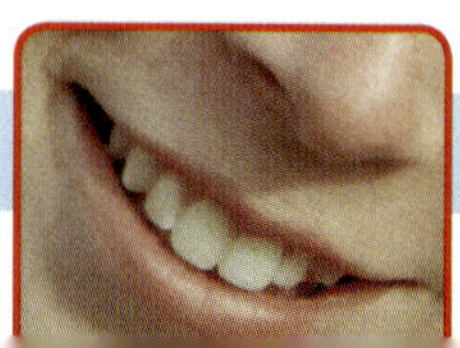

Becoming older

Track 49

AH

Paul, Emily, Carla and Cem are sitting in the new ice-cream parlour. They are having their ice creams. They're talking about their future.

Being a pupil at school is fun, usually. But there comes a time after school. You're probably looking forward to that moment when you graduate. But what comes after school? Have you thought about that yet?

Many adults say you're responsible for whatever you do and of course for whatever you don't do. You must know which job you would like to do. You must know what you're interested in and what you're not interested in.

Later as an adult you have more rights, but you also have more obligations. Maybe being at school isn't that bad after all.

P

1. Read the text. What are the main aspects of the text?
2. Do you agree with the text?
   Say: *I agree because I think it's important to know what I want in life.*
   I don't agree because I don't want to think about the future yet.
3. The text says something about rights and obligations as an adult. What are they? Make a list and write it into a table:

rights as an adult	obligations as an adult
I can watch what I want on TV. …	I must go to work to have money. …

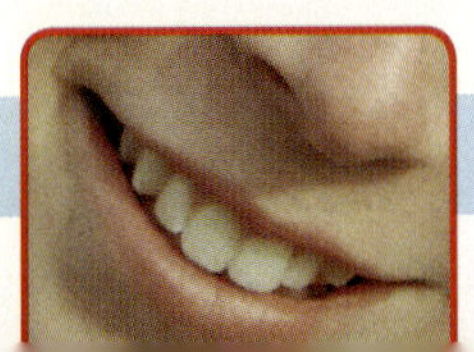

Everyday life

Track 50

AH

Emily is at home with her parents. She tells them all about the talk with Paul, Carla and Cem. Now Emily is talking with her parents about life as an adult.

Dad: "Look, Emily this is our rental contract for the flat."

Emily: "That looks very complicated."

Mum: "It's OK. But you must read it carefully before you sign it."

Emily: "Which other contracts do you have here?"

Dad: "This is my employment contract."

Mum: "And here's a subscription for a magazine that we get every week."

Emily: "I suppose I must read all that on my own and fill in many forms when I grow up."

Dad: "Even when you want a mobile phone, you must fill in a form and sign it. When you marry, you must fill in a form and sign it. When you apply for a job, you must fill in a form and sign it."

Emily: "So life is all about forms?"

Mum: "Well, not completely. But you need a lot of forms. And you must keep them in a file like we have. That's very important because you are responsible for everything you do and everything you sign."

1. Read the dialogue. Summarise.
2. What do **you** think? Which information must you give when you fill in a form?
3. Which forms do you know? Think of banks, subscriptions or forms you find online. Collect.
4. Form teams. Go out and collect forms from different public services.

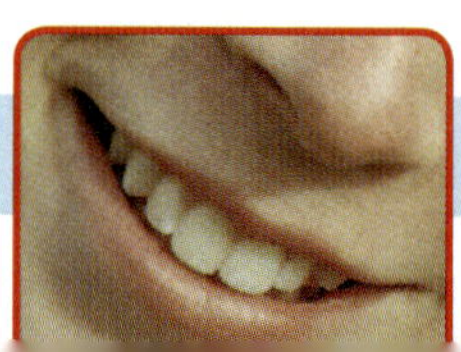

What if there is a problem?

Track 51

AH

When you have a problem help is not always “around the corner”. Then what can you do?

You can use your mobile phone and contact the local authorities. You can contact the police, the fire brigade or call an ambulance for medical help.

Each country has its own emergency number or several emergency numbers.

Germany has the numbers 110 and 112. But which number is for the police and which number is for an ambulance or the fire brigade?

In Great Britain, there is only one emergency number. It’s 999 for the police, the fire brigade and for an ambulance.

1. Listen to the CD and read along.
2. Look at the picture. What must you do when you see an accident? Say: *When I see an accident I must …*

7 Around town:

Witnessing an accident

Track 82

AH

Paul and Emily have just witnessed an accident. The police are there. They want to question the two friends.

Police: "Hello, you two. Did you see how the accident happened?"

Paul: "Yes, we did. The blue car came from over there. It was next to the garage."

Police: "What happened then?"

Emily: "The other car was opposite the junction. It was at the traffic lights."

Police: "Where was the blue car then?"

Emily: "The blue car was at the traffic lights, too."

Police: "Did it wait at the traffic lights?"

Paul: "No, it didn't. It went right across the junction and hit the blue car just in front of the driver."

Police: "That was a good description. Thank you very much."

Paul and Emily: "You're welcome, Sir."

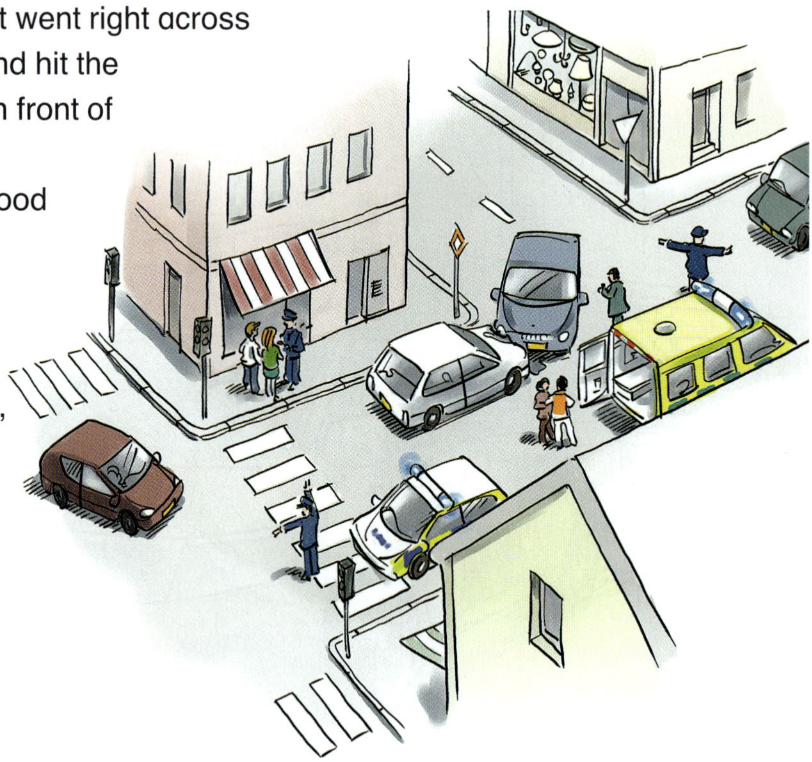

gr

1. Read the text and listen to the CD.
2. Act the scene.
3. Think of another accident.

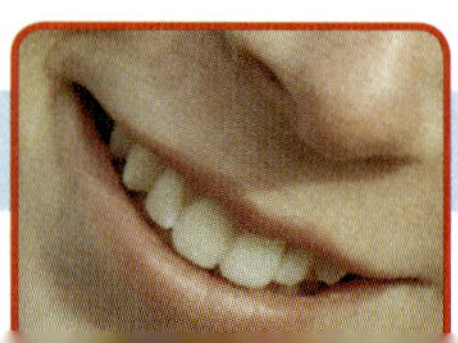

A musical digression: "Help"

Track 53

When I was younger, so much younger than today,
I never needed anybody's help in any way.
But now these days are gone, I'm not so self assured,
Now I find I've changed my mind and opened up the doors.

Help me if you can, I'm feeling down
And I do appreciate you being round.
Help me, get my feet back on the ground,
Won't you please, please help me?

And now my life has changed in oh so many ways,
My independence seems to vanish in the haze.
But every now and then I feel so insecure,
I know that I just need you like I've never done before.

This is a cover of the LP "Help".

Help me if you can, I'm feeling down
And I do appreciate you being round.
Help me, get my feet back on the ground,
Won't you please, please help me.

When I was younger, so much younger than today,
I never needed anybody's help in any way.
But now these days are gone, I'm not so self assured,
Now I find I've changed my mind and opened up the doors.

Help me if you can, I'm feeling down
And I do appreciate you being round.
Help me, get my feet back on the ground,
Won't you please, please help me, help me, help me, oh.

1. Listen to the song.
2. Read the lyrics of the song.
3. Can you say what the song is about?
   Say: *The song is about …*

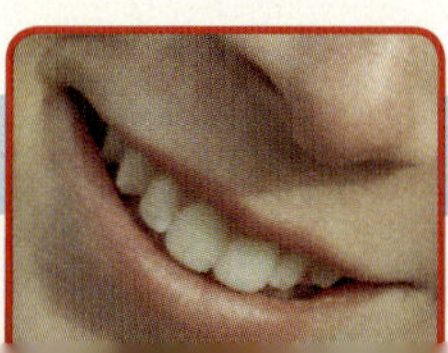

über den Inhalt eines Liedtextes sprechen

Strategy: Step by step

In the event of an accident you must do certain things.
You must answer certain questions when you call an ambulance, for example.

1. Put the pictures into the correct order. Write what the speaker says into a list.
2. Answer all the questions. Use the text *“Witnessing an accident”* to practise.
3. Do an *“emergency role-play”*.

P

This is what you have learned

Quiz: In emergencies

1. **Form two teams.**
2. **Each team rolls a dice.**
3. **The team to reach the higher score may answer the first question.**
4. **The tasks are:**
   - **a.** You want to know how many people are injured. What do you ask?
   - **b.** Name three further questions in an emergency call.
   - **c.** You have lost your wallet or your purse. Where do you go?
   - **d.** You want to know where the accident happened. What do you ask?
   - **e.** What are the German emergency numbers? Name both.
   - **f.** What is the emergency number in Great Britain?
   - **g.** Name an obligation as an adult.
   - **h.** Name a right as an adult.
5. **The team to answer more questions wins the quiz.**

Well, how did you do? ☺

8 Around the world:

Track 56

United States of America

- *Statue of Liberty*
- *Empire State Building*
- *The White House*
- *Grand Canyon*
- *Niagara Falls*
- *Mt. Rushmore*
- *Yellowstone National Park*
- *Golden Gate Bridge*
- *Hollywood*
- *Las Vegas*

AH

Plan your journey to the US

New York City

Empire State Building – *Highest skyscraper in New York (381m, 102 floors, 73 lifts and 1860 steps)*

Statue of Liberty *(symbol of freedom)*

Manhattan *(more skyscrapers)*

Broadway *(theatres and musicals)*

There are lots of things to see and do in New York. I must go shopping.

Washington D.C. – The White House

The President of the United States of America lives here.

Washington is the capital of the United States of America. There are more interesting historical things to see.

Niagara Falls

Very big waterfalls at the border between the US and Canada. The water falls down 52 metres on the Canadian side. You can go on a boat trip to see the falls.

The word means "thundering water" in the Native American language.

Mount Rushmore

The heads of the four most important presidents of the United States (Washington, Jefferson, Roosevelt, Lincoln) are carved into the stone. The heads are 18.3 metres high. Wow! They used dynamite to make the heads.

Las Vegas

It's in the middle of the desert. In this city there are a lot of casinos. But I can't gamble there because I am not 21 years old. Some hotels look like famous buildings: you can find the Eiffel tower, Castle Neuschwanstein, an Egyptian pyramid and even a small Statue of Liberty there.

8 Around the world:

The Grand Canyon

It is one of the most impressive sights in the US. The canyon is 450 km long, between 6 and 30 km wide and up to 1800 metres deep. The Colorado river flows at the bottom of the canyon and you can go rafting there. I'd love to do that.

San Francisco – Golden Gate Bridge

It's not the longest bridge in the US but it is one of the most beautiful bridges in the world. It is 2737 metres long. 120000 cars and other vehicles cross the bridge every day.

San Francisco is an interesting city. The Gold Rush in California started here and in the Sixties the city was the Hippie capital of the world.

1. Read Paul's texts.
2. These numbers are from the description of the sights. Which sight is it and what do the numbers mean?
   18.3 * 120000 * 1860 * 52 * 21 * 450
3. Which sights would you like to visit? Why?
4. Paul has not finished his research yet. Use the internet to find out about the missing sights: Hollywood and Yellowstone National Park.
5. What is the most interesting sight in your city or area? Find a picture and make notes or write a short text like Paul did.

P

Fact file USA

AH

name:	*United States of America*
capital:	*Washington D.C.*
President:	*Barack Obama (since 2009)*
public holiday:	*Independence Day (4th of July)*
size:	*9.83 million km²*
population:	*308 million*
borders:	*Canada (north), Mexico (south)*
states:	*50*
currency:	*US Dollar*
official language:	*English*
other languages:	*Spanish, Native American languages*
nationality:	*American*
highest mountain:	*Mount McKinley (Alaska)*
longest river:	*Mississippi*
largest city:	*New York*

gr

1. Answer the following questions:
   - What is the capital of the United States?
   - When is the national holiday?
   - Who is the president of the United States?
   - How many states are there in the United States?
   - What are the languages of the United States?
2. Add more questions. Ask your partner.

What When Where Who	is are	the currency the longest river the highest mountain the largest city the borders	of the United States?

3. Can you answer these questions for Germany? Use the internet to find the answers.

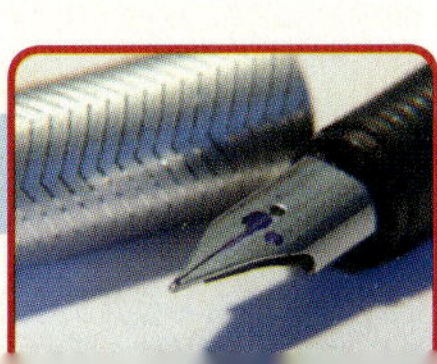

At the airport

Track 59

AH

Ground staff: "Good morning."
Paul: "Good morning."
Ground staff: "Where are you going today?"
Paul: "I'm travelling to New York."
Ground staff: "Could I have your ticket and your passport, please?"
Paul: "Here you are."
Ground staff: "Thank you. Would you like a window or an aisle seat?"
Paul: "An aisle seat, please."
Ground staff: "Do you have any luggage?"
Paul: "Yes, this suitcase and this small bag."

Ground staff:
"Put your suitcase on the scales, please. OK, that's 19 kilos. Do you want to take the small bag as hand baggage?"
Paul: "Yes, I do."
Ground staff:
"Here's your boarding card. Boarding starts at 10.20 from gate 25. Have a nice flight."
Paul: "Thank you."

1. Listen to the dialogue.
2. Practise reading the dialogue with a partner.
3. Write a new dialogue. Use this information:
   San Francisco – window seat – two suitcases and a daypack – 28 kilos – at 6.45 from gate 18b

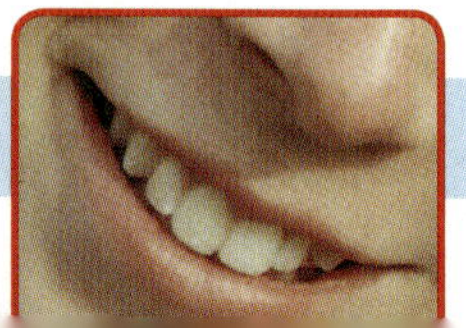

Same language – different words

Track 61

AH

What's the problem? Paul and his aunt both speak English. Why doesn't Paul's aunt understand him?
Sometimes the same thing has different names in America and in Great Britain. Here are a few examples:

BE	AE
boot	trunk
cinema	movie-theatre
petrol	gas
sweets	candy
taxi	cab
football	soccer
trousers	pants
lorry	truck

British English

American English

BE	AE
chips	French fries
flat	apartment
pub	bar
pavement	sidewalk
underground	subway
lift	elevator
biscuits	cookies
autumn	fall

1. Listen to Paul and his aunt saying these words.
2. Practise with a partner. One says the British English word, the other says the American English word.

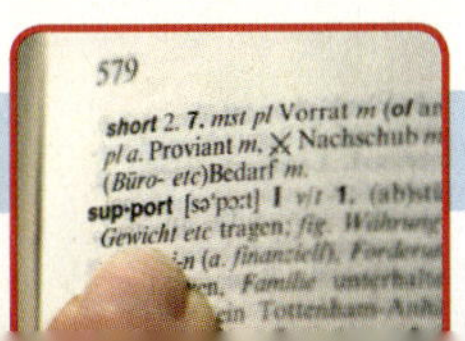

Postcards from the United States

Track 64

Hi Emily,

I'm in the USA now. First I flew to New York. There I met my aunt and my cousin Toby. We made a boat tour to see the Statue of Liberty and the skyline of Manhattan. We also went to the top of the Empire State Building.

Then we went to Washington to see the White House. I wanted to see the President but I didn't. Next we drove to the Niagara Falls at the Canadian border. I got very wet on the boat. We're still at the Niagara falls but will fly to Los Angeles tomorrow.

Love, Paul XXX

To
Emily Jones
3 College Road, Clifton
BRISTOL
BS8 3HA

UNITED KINGDOM

Hi Emily,

Now we're in San Francisco. My aunt, Toby and I flew to Los Angeles yesterday. We went to Hollywood and visited the famous film studios. Today we drove on to San Francisco where we'll stay for two more days. Then we're driving to the Grand Canyon and maybe stop at Las Vegas on our way. It's a long drive. America is so big, you can't see everything in one holiday. I must come back next year. Maybe you want to come with me.

Love, PAUL XXX

To
Emily Jones
3 College Road, Clifton
BRISTOL
BS8 3HA

UNITED KINGDOM

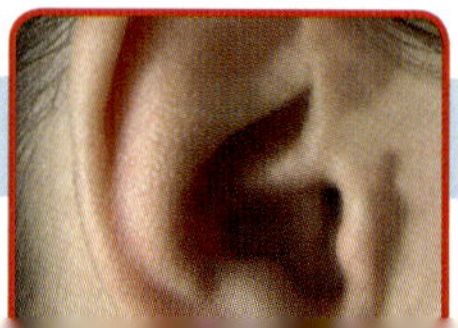

1. Read the texts and write up Paul's journey through the USA.
   Write: *1st stop: New York*   *2nd stop: …*
2. Now listen to Paul telling Emily about his journey after he's back in England.
   Write: *1st stop: New York*   *2nd stop: …*
3. Compare the two lists. Paul has made a few mistakes. Can you find them?
4. Look at the pictures on p. 82/83 and at the texts. Imagine you have been on a journey to the United States. Where did **you** go to?
   Write: *First I went to New York.*   *Then …*

First Then Next	I went I flew I drove …	to New York. to the Grand Canyon. …

5. Write a postcard to a friend from your trip.
   - Where did you go?
   - Who was with you?
   - When did you go?
   - What did you see there?
   - What did you do there?

P

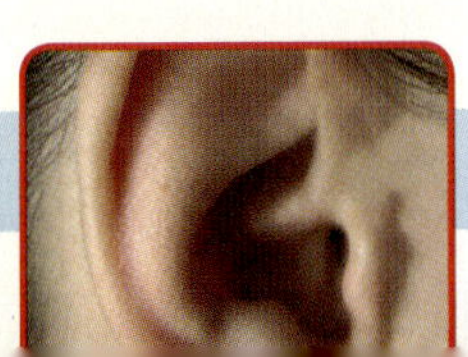

8 Around the world:

Strategy: Reading a table

This is a table. Not a table you can sit or eat at but one you can use to show information in a very simple way. Once you learn to read a table it can be very helpful for you. A table is made from rows and columns.

1. Find the title of the table. It tells you what the table is about.
2. Look at the first row and column of every table. They tell you what information you can find.
3. Now find the place where the row and the column meet. Here you can find the information you want.

Geographical information

	United States	Great Britain	Australia
Capital	Washington	London	Canberra
Largest city	New York	London	Sydney
Longest river	Mississippi	Thames	Darling
Highest mountain	Mount McKinley	Ben Nevis	Mount Kosciusko

1. Look at the table. What is it about?
2. What is the longest river in Great Britain? Find the row “longest river” and the column “Great Britain”.
3. Copy the table into your exercise book and add the column “Germany”.
4. Fill in the missing information about Germany.

This is what you have learned

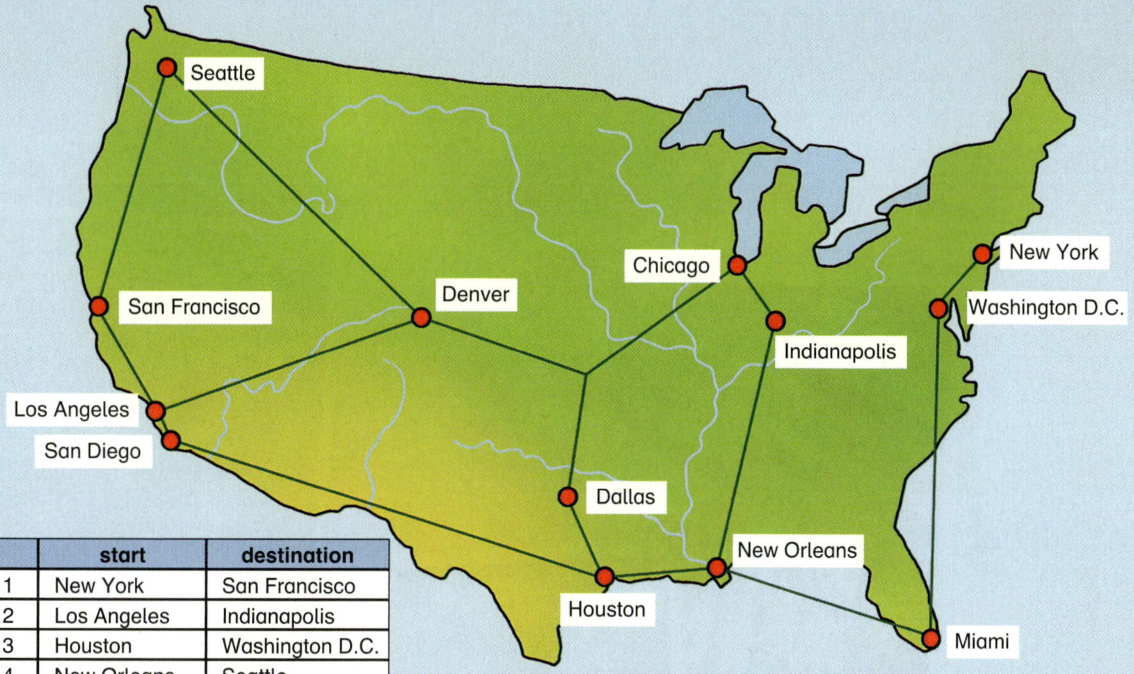

	start	destination
1	New York	San Francisco
2	Los Angeles	Indianapolis
3	Houston	Washington D.C.
4	New Orleans	Seattle
5	Chicago	San Diego
6	Denver	Miami

This is how you play

You need two dice and a token for each player.

1. Make a list of twenty questions about the USA. Keep the questions secret.
2. Then find a partner and start your journey through the USA.
3. Take two dice and roll them two times.
   - First roll: This is the city you start at – your starting point.
   - Second roll: This is the city you must go to – your destination.
4. Put your token on your starting point.
5. Answer one of your partner's questions.
   - Have you got the correct answer? Move to the next city on your way to your destination.
   - You don't know the answer? You must stay at the city you're in at the moment.
6. Now it's your partner's turn.
7. Who is first at his or her destination?

9 Around the year:

Track 65

Memorial Day and Independence Day

Memorial Day

- *a war*
- *an enemy*
- *a memorial*
- *to remember*
- *to attack*
- *to fight*
- *a soldier*
- *a parade*
- *United States of America*
- *last Monday in May*

Independence Day

- *independence*
- *stripes*
- *stars*
- *a flag*
- *history*
- *fireworks*
- *a barbecue*
- *a national anthem*
- *4th of July*

Memorial Day

Track 66

AH

Paul:
"Hey Grandpa, I need your help. I need some information about Memorial Day for a presentation at school with Emily."

Grandfather:
"There's lots to tell … I was in the Vietnam war for about two years from 1965 to 1966. My best friend Jack was with me. I was glad to have him with me because it was the most horrible time of my life. Five days before we were sent back home to America, we were attacked by the enemy and Jack was killed … since then I have had nightmares."

Paul: "… Oh! … How did you feel when you came back to America?"

Grandfather: "Well, the first soldiers coming back to America were celebrated. I was one of the last soldiers. When we came back almost nobody cared about us. Every year on the last Monday in May, I think of Jack and all the others who lost their lives in a war."

1. Look up what "memorial" means.
2. Listen to the CD and read along.
3. Why is it important to remember war?
   Say: *It's important to remember war because …*
4. Is there a similar day in your country?
5. What can you do to avoid war?

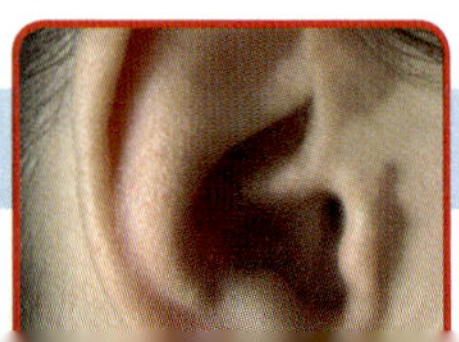

A poster presentation

Track 67

AH

Emily and Paul need a poster for their presentation at school with the most important facts about Memorial Day.

Hey Paul, I've already made the poster.

I'm sorry, Emily. The information is **not** correct. In 2009 Memorial Day is on the 25th of May. It's to remember soldiers who lost their lives in war. It's not celebrated in Africa, it's celebrated in America. Where did you get the information from?

I found it on the internet, so it **must be** correct.

But Emily, you should keep in mind that there may be incorrect information on the internet. **Everybody** can write things on the internet. It's not checked by anybody, so you should always be careful. And Emily … the poster looks boring without pictures.

1. Listen to the CD and read along.
2. Why did Emily write incorrect information on the poster?
3. Read the strategy on page 98.

9 Around the year:

Strategy: Working with search engines

Looking for information

a. Go to a search engine like www.google.co.uk.
b. Type in your keywords.
c. Click on "Google Search".
For further details take a quick look at page 13.

➔ **There is some incorrect information:**
Check several homepages to make sure you get the correct information.

Looking for pictures

a. Go to a search engine like www.google.co.uk.
b. Click on "Images".
c. Type in your keywords.
d. Click on "Google Search".

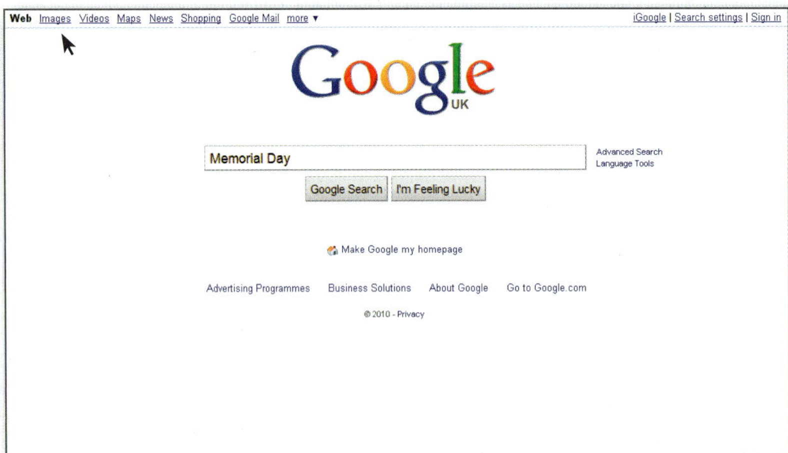

1. Which search engines do you know?
2. Where do **you** type in your keywords?
3. Look for correct information about Memorial Day on the internet. Look for pictures, too.

Independence Day

Track 70

AH

Independence Day is a public holiday in the United States of America. On the 4th of July 1776, America declared its independence from Great Britain. It was the beginning of the history of the United States of America. Every year on the 4th of July, there are big parades in every village, town and city. People enjoy having picnics and barbecues or they go on trips to the beach or to the countryside. And in the evening there are fireworks to celebrate the birthday of the United States of America.

1. Listen to the CD and read along.
2. Is there a similar public holiday in your country? Make a presentation about it.

P

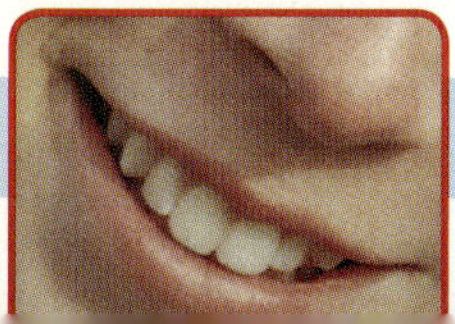

9 Around the year:

How Francis Scott Key wrote the national anthem

Track 71

In 1814 Francis Scott Key was held on a ship. He knew the British would attack America during the night.
He was scared. And he didn't want the British to win because that would mean that America wouldn't be independent anymore.

During the night the British did come to attack America. There was a fight between the British and the Americans.

When Francis Scott Key woke up in the morning, he was afraid that the British had won. And he was afraid the American flag wouldn't be there anymore. So he ran on deck of the ship to have a look:

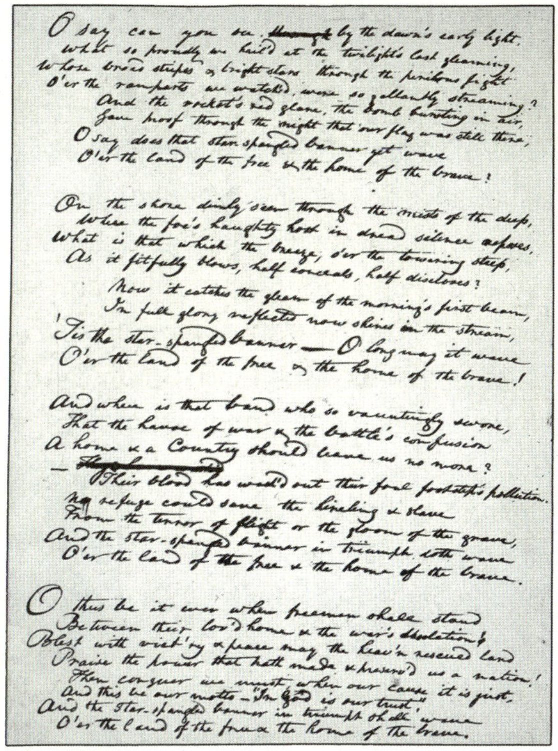

O say can you see by the dawn's early light
What so proudly we hail'd at the twilight's last gleaming,
Whose broad stripes & bright stars through the perilous fight
O'er the ramparts we watch'd, were so gallantly streaming?
And the rocket's red glare, the bomb bursting in air,
Gave proof through the night that our flag was still there,
O say does that star-spangled banner yet wave
O'er the land of the free & the home of the brave?

On the shore dimly seen through the mists of the deep,
Where the foe's haughty host in dread silence reposes,
What is that which the breeze, o'er the towering steep,
As it fitfully blows, half conceals, half discloses?
Now it catches the gleam of the morning's first beam,
In full glory reflected now shines in the stream,
'Tis the star-spangled banner — O long may it wave
O'er the land of the free & the home of the brave!

And where is that band who so vauntingly swore,
That the havoc of war & the battle's confusion
A home & a Country should leave us no more?
— Their blood has wash'd out their foul footstep's pollution.
No refuge could save the hireling & slave
From the terror of flight or the gloom of the grave,
And the star-spangled banner in triumph doth wave
O'er the land of the free & the home of the brave.

O thus be it ever when freemen shall stand
Between their lov'd home & the war's desolation!
Blest with vict'ry & peace may the heav'n rescued land
Praise the power that hath made & preserv'd us a nation!
Then conquer we must, when our cause it is just,
And this be our motto — "In God is our trust,"
And the star-spangled banner in triumph shall wave
O'er the land of the free & the home of the brave.

The flag still waved over the land. Francis Scott Key was very proud to be an American and he was very happy that America was still independent. He was so glad that he immediately sat down to write a poem. Much later, on the 3rd of March, 1931, this poem became the national anthem of the United States of America.

1. Listen to the CD and read along.
2. Who wrote the text for the national anthem of America?
3. Why did he write it?
4. Find out about other national anthems:
   - Who wrote them?
   - And why?
   - What are they about?

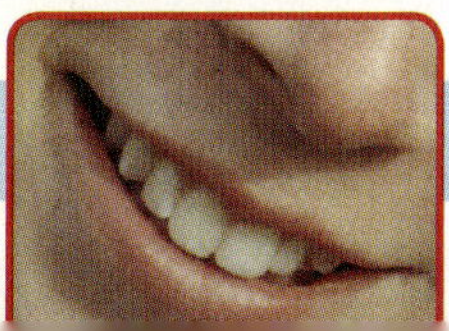

Track 72

The national anthem of America

The Star-Spangled Banner

AH

The American national anthem is also called "The Star-Spangled Banner" because it's about the American flag. The flag has changed over the years. The current American flag has thirteen stripes and fifty stars. When the United States of America were founded, there were only thirteen states: Delaware, Pennsylvania, New Jersey, Georgia, Connecticut, Massachusetts, Maryland, South Carolina, New Hampshire, Virginia, New York, North Carolina and Rhode Island. The stripes stand for those states. Each time a state joined the United States of America, a star was added on the flag. The 50th star was added in 1960 when Hawaii became part of the United States. When Americans sing their national anthem, most of them stand up, look at the flag and touch their heart.

1777

Today

Track 73

1. Listen to the American national anthem.
2. Look at the American flag.
   - How many stars are there? What do they stand for?
   - How many stripes are there? What do they stand for?

This is what you have learned

Which picture belongs to which holiday?

10 Life after school:

Track 74

In the future I will …

- *voluntary work*
- *a job*
- *an application*
- *to apply*
- *a letter*
- *an old people's home*
- *an animal shelter*
- *the future*
- *graduation*
- *to graduate*
- *a waitress*
- *a bus driver*

Graduation – and then?

Track 75

Emily and her best friend Carla are sitting in the living room. It's the week before their graduation.

Emily: "I wonder what life will be like after school."

Carla: "What are your plans for the future, Emily?"

Emily: "Well, I think I'm going to find a job as a waitress. And I'm going to marry Paul."

Carla: "Are you going to have kids?"

Emily: "Yes. I'd like to have three kids, two girls and a boy. And we're going to have a gold fish and a dog, of course. I like dogs."

Carla: "Where are you going to live?"

Emily: "I think we're going to live in a nice flat in Manchester so we can be close to my grandparents and take care of them when they need us."

Carla: "Hey, let's write letters to ourselves. Let's write about our life in five years."

Emily: "Great idea. We won't open them until then and find out if our dreams have become true."

gr

1. Read the text, listen to the CD and read along.
2. What are **your** plans for the future? Discuss in class.

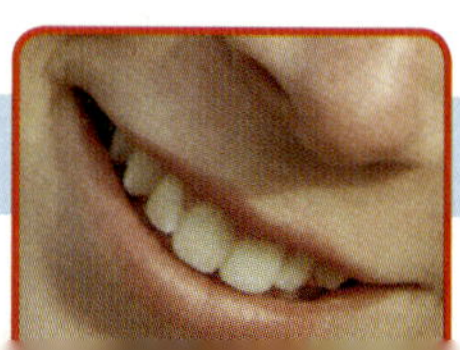

Carla's letter

Track 76

Dear Carla-in-five-years,

It's the week before graduation. I'm so nervous about graduating because I don't have a job yet and I don't know what I'm going to do with my free time. But I think I'll have a job in five years. I think I'll be a popstar. Right now, I'm in love with Cem but I don't think he knows. But maybe he'll be my boyfriend. And I think I'll live in my own house in Bristol and I'm going to have two cats. I would like to have two children, a boy and a girl. Their na-mes will be Tom and Paulina. I hope my dreams will become true.

Carla

1. Read Carla's letter.
2. Write a letter to yourself. Talk about your plans for the future and about your life in five years.

AH

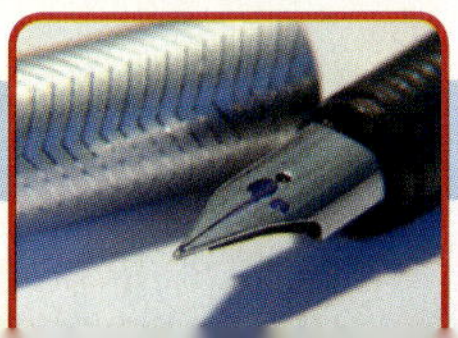

Track 77

AH

A musical digression: "Qué Será, Será – what will be, will be"

When I was just a little girl
I asked my mother, what will I be
Will I be pretty, will I be rich
Here's what she said to me.

Qué Será, Será,
Whatever will be, will be
The future's not ours, to see
Qué Será, Será
What will be, will be.

This is a photo of Doris Day.

When I grew up and fell in love
I asked my sweetheart what lies ahead
Will we have rainbows, day after day
Here's what my sweetheart said.

Qué Será, Será,
Whatever will be, will be
The future's not ours, to see
Qué Será, Será
What will be, will be.

Now I have children of my own
They ask their mother, what will I be
Will I be handsome, will I be rich
I tell them tenderly.

Qué Será, Será,
Whatever will be, will be
The future's not ours, to see
Qué Será, Será
What will be, will be.

1. Before you listen to the song: Look at the title. What is the song about? What do you think?
2. While you are listening to the song: Read along.
3. After listening to the song:
   - Your friends want to know what the song is about. What do you tell them?
   - What does the question "Will we have rainbows, day after day" in line 12 mean? What do you think? Discuss in class.

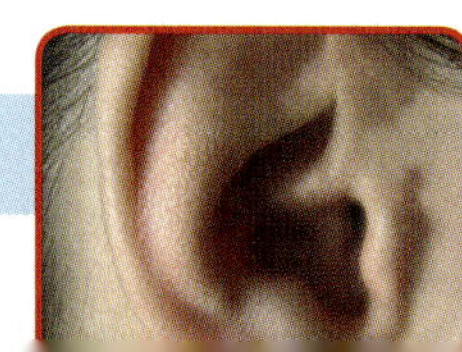

Paul does not have a job yet

Track 78

Paul has graduated from school but he doesn't have a job yet. He has applied for several jobs but he still can't find one. Paul is very sad. His friends have come to talk to him.

Carla: "What's the matter with you, Paul?"

Paul: "Well, I've written so many applications but nobody wants to give me a job."

Emily: "I'm sure you'll find a job soon."

Paul: "But what if I don't? What am I going to do? Everyone has a job. I don't want to sit at home and wait for a job."

Cem: "But you shouldn't give up hope. You should continue writing applications."

Emily: "And in the meantime, you could do some voluntary work. You wouldn't have to sit at home and wait but you could do something."

Paul: "Voluntary work?"

Carla: "I think that's a good idea."

Emily: "Yes, you could help people for example in an old people's home."

Ben: "Let's go and find out about voluntary work on the internet."

1. Act the scene.
2. What do you think about Emily's idea? Discuss in class.
3. Can you think of other ways to help Paul? What would **you** do in his situation?

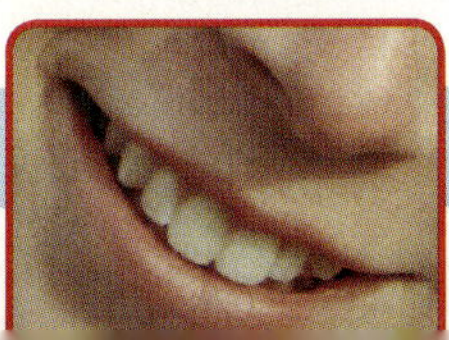

die eigene Meinung darstellen

Do you like animals?

Track 79

Do you like animals?

You don't know what to do in your free time?
Our animals need you!
Please volunteer at the animal shelter.

For example, you could take the dogs for a walk.
Or you could help clean the cages and feed the animals.

For more information please call Brenda on 01604 12345.

Would you like to make someone happy?

Do you want to do something useful in your free time?

Please volunteer at the old people's home.

For example, you could read a book to someone. Or you could play games with old people.

For more information please call Tom on 01503 98765.

1. Read the voluntary work offers. Where would **you** like to work?
2. Find websites on the internet.

Looking for voluntary work

Track 80

AH

Everybody is trying to help Paul to find voluntary work.

Paul, I think you should work at an old people's home because you could make many people happy. The old people will be very happy when you read to them or play with them. Sometimes they don't have many visitors. And you are good with people. I think you would enjoy working there.

I think you should work at the animal shelter because you love animals. You could play with the animals all day long. You would keep fit because you would take the dogs for a walk and clean the cages.

I think Paul should work at a charity shop because he can get work experience there. Then he could apply for other jobs in a shop. And he would meet many interesting people.

1. Listen to the text and read along.
2. Why should Paul work there?
   Say: *Paul should work at an old people's home/animal shelter/at a charity shop because …*
3. Where would **you** like to work? Why?
   Say: *I would like to work (at a charity shop) because …*
4. Where would **you** not like to work? Why?
   Say: *I would not like to work (at a charity shop) because …*

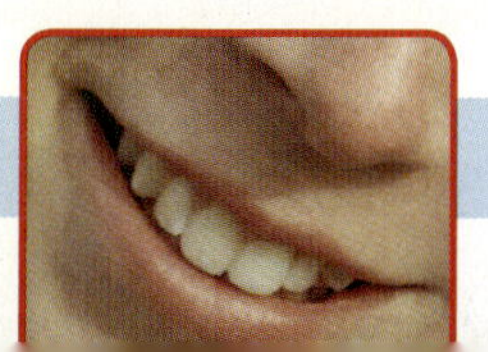

Strategy: Learning English after school

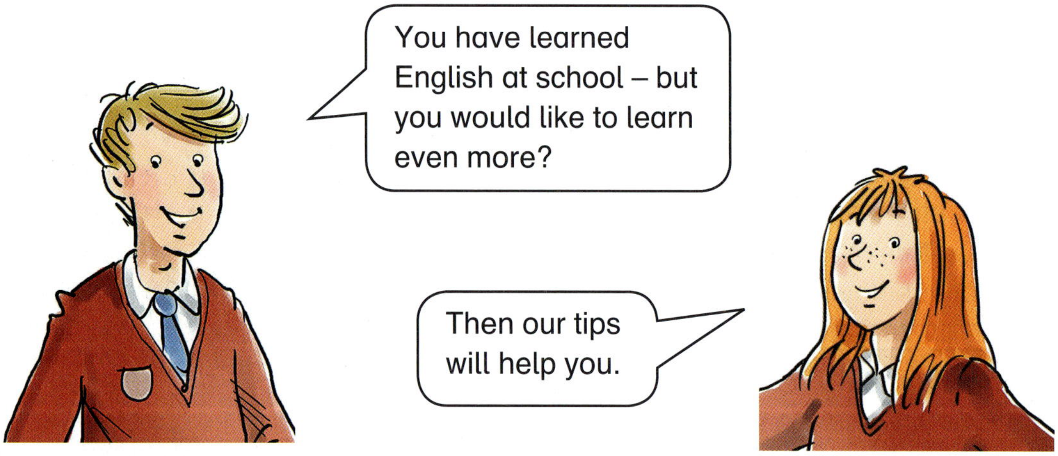

You could ...

... listen to English songs.
... read newspapers and magazines in English.
... watch TV in English.
... listen to English radio stations.
... go to your community college (Volkshochschule).
... write e-mails with someone from England, Canada, USA, ...

1. What else could you do to learn English after school?
2. Look for local English courses.

This is what you have learned

Track 83

AH

Listen to the song and sing along.
Find out what the song is about. Use your dictionary.

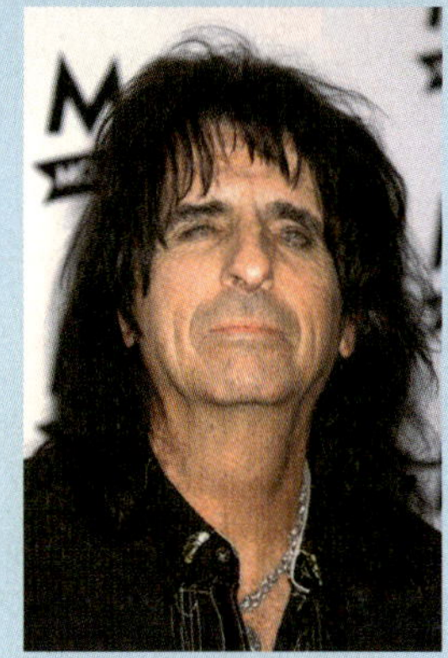

This is a photo of Alice Cooper.

A musical digression: “School’s out”

Well we got no choice
All the girls and boys
Makin’ all that noise
’Cause they found new toys
Well we can’t salute ya
Can’t find a flag
If that don’t suit ya
That’s a drag

School’s out for summer
School’s out forever
School’s been blown to pieces

No more pencils
No more books
No more teacher’s dirty looks

Well we got no class
And we got no principles
We ain’t got no innocence
We can’t even think of a word that rhymes

School’s out for summer
School’s out forever
My school’s been blown to pieces

No more pencils
No more books
No more teacher’s dirty looks

Out for summer
Out ’til fall
We might not come back at all

School’s out forever
School’s out for summer
School’s out with fever
School’s out completely

School’s out forever!

11 Grammar:

To play with language

11 Grammar:

To play with language – mit Sprache spielen

Jedes Spiel folgt bestimmten Spielregeln. Diese Spielregeln musst du kennen und beachten, damit das Spiel funktioniert. Ähnlich ist es mit den Sprachen. Die englische Sprache folgt bestimmten Regeln, der Grammatik. Wenn du diese Regeln kennst, fällt es dir leichter, eine Sprache zu lernen.

Auf den folgenden Seiten findest du zunächst einige Sprachforscher-Aufgaben (S. 118), um mit Sprache zu spielen und die Spielregeln der englischen Sprache kennen zu lernen.

Im Anschluss findest du eine Zusammenfassung der Sprachregeln (S. 123): die englische Grammatik.

Folgende Tabelle hilft dir, schwierige Wörter besser zu verstehen.

Deutsch	Fachbegriff	Englisch
Befehlsform	Imperativ	imperative
Besitzanzeigendes Fürwort	Possessivpronomen	possessiv pronoun
Besitzfall (Wesfall mit 's)	s-Genitiv	s-genitive
Eigenschaftswort (Wiewort)	Adjektiv	adjective
einfache Form der Gegenwart	einfaches Präsens	simple present
einfache Form der Vergangenheit	einfaches Präteritum	simple past
Einzahl	Singular	singular
Entscheidungsfragen		Yes/No questions
Fragen mit Fragewörtern (Bestimmungsfragen)		questions with question words
Gegenwart	Präsens	present tense
Grundform	Infinitiv	infinitive
Hauptwort (Namenwort)	Nomen (Substantiv)	noun
Hilfsverb	Auxiliarverb (Modalverb)	auxiliary verb

Deutsch	Fachbegriff	Englisch
Kurzform		short form
Langform		long form
Mehrzahl	Plural	plural
Fürwort	Objektpronomen	
persönliches Fürwort	Personalpronomen	personal pronoun
Tätigkeitswort (Tuwort, Zeitwort)	Verb	verb
unbestimmtes Umstandswort der Zeit	Zeitadverb, Adverbien der Häufigkeit	adverbs of indefinite time
Vergangenheit	Präteritum	past tense
Verhältniswort	Präposition	preposition
	Ortspräpositionen	prepositions of place
	Richtungspräpositionen	prepositions of direction
Verlaufsform der Gegenwart (-ing-Form)		present progressive
Verlaufsform als Satzobjekt	Gerundium	gerund
Vollendete Gegenwart	Perfekt	present perfect
Zukunft	Futur	future tense
Zukunft mit going to		going to-future
Zukunft mit will		will-future

Sprachforscher-Aufgaben

1. Lies dir im **ersten Kapitel** (Modern communication) die Texte "E-pals" durch. Schreibe alle Sätze heraus, in denen gesagt wird, ob die Jugendlichen etwas mögen oder nicht. Schreibe die Sätze untereinander in dein Heft. Unterstreiche das Verb in jedem Satz. Unterstreiche die Verlaufsform (-ing-Form) mit einer anderen Farbe.

2. Schreibe drei Dinge auf, die du magst. Unterstreiche wieder das Verb und die Verlaufsform in den gewählten Farben.
   Schreibe drei Dinge auf, die du nicht magst. Unterstreiche auch hier wieder.

3. Jetzt kannst du mithilfe der Farben und der Beispielsätze selbst kontrollieren, ob du alles richtig gemacht hast.

4. Sammelt in einer Gruppe auf einem Poster alle -ing-Formen und schreibt die Grundform des dazugehörigen Verbs daneben.
   Könnt ihr Regeln zur Bildung der -ing-Form ableiten?

5. Schau dir im ersten Kapitel die Seite "Get Smart" an. Hier lernst du Worte kennen, mit denen du sagen kannst, wie häufig man etwas tut.
   Welche sind das und wie kann man sie übersetzen?

6. Schreibe (natürlich in Englisch) auf, wie häufig du Folgendes tust:
   - ein Buch lesen
   - Fußball spielen
   - Musik hören
   - Essen für deine Eltern kochen
   - fernsehen
   - einkaufen gehen

   Fällt dir noch mehr ein? Vergleiche mit einem Nachbarn.

7. Im **zweiten Kapitel** (Shopping) geht es um das gemeinsame Einkaufen.
   Schau dir den Dialog auf S. 20 (decisions) genau an.
   Hier sprechen alle über verschiedene Pullover. Trotzdem wird das Wort Pullover selten benutzt. Wie wird das Wort Pullover ersetzt? Wie würde man das im Deutschen sagen?

8. Im **zweiten Kapitel** findest du viele Adjektive (Eigenschaftswörter), die nicht nur in der Grundform abgebildet sind, sondern auch verändert.
Zum Beispiel: big, bigger, biggest.
Suche auf S. 20 alle Wörter heraus, die du findest. Übertrage diese Tabelle in dein Heft und vervollständige sie.

Grundform	1. Steigerung	2. Steigerung
big	bigger	biggest
expensive		
pretty		
...		

9. Im **dritten Kapitel** (Love and friendship) werden Regeln für die erste Verabredung aufgestellt (Seite 32). Diese werden in der Befehlsform (Imperativ) formuliert. Schaue dir jeweils das Verb im Satz genau an:
   - An welcher Stelle im Satz steht es?
   - Welche Form wird benutzt?
   - Was passiert bei der Verneinung?

10. Im **dritten Kapitel** werden Personen miteinander verglichen. Suche aus dem Dialog "Matchmaking" (Seite 33) die Sätze mit Adjektiven (Eigenschaftswörtern) heraus und schreibe sie auf.
    - Unterstreiche die Adjektive.
    - Vergleiche. Was stellst du fest?
    - Welche Wörter stehen in Verbindung mit den Adjektiven?
    - Welche Vergleichsform benutzt du

    – wenn sich zwei Menschen voneinander unterscheiden?

    – wenn zwei Menschen in einem Punkt gleich sind?

11. Im **vierten Kapitel** (Lifestyle and fashion) sollst du deine Meinung zu Outfits äußern.
Warum gefällt dir welches Outfit? Schreibe vier Sätze in dein Heft.
Verwende die Bindewörter (Konjunktionen) *or, and, but* und/oder *because.*
Unterstreiche die Bindewörter in deinen Sätzen.

12. Wenn du deutlich machen möchtest, dass jemandem etwas gehört oder jemand einer Gruppe angehört, wendest du das Genitiv-s an:

*This is Susan'**s** bike.*	Dies ist Susan**s** Fahrrad.
*Tom'**s** father is very friendly.*	Tom**s** Vater ist sehr freundlich.

Blättere in diesem Buch und finde einige Beispiele für das Genitiv-s. Beginne mit dem **fünften Kapitel** (Experiencing work). Schreibe die Beispiele in dein Heft, schreibe die entsprechende Seitenzahl daneben und vergleiche deine Ergebnisse mit deinem Sitznachbarn.

Wenn das Bezugswort eine Ortsangabe ist wie zum Beispiel *house, flat* oder *shop*, wird dieses Wort meist weggelassen:

*At the Nelson'**s**.* (anstelle von: *At the Nelson'**s** house.*)	Bei den Nelsons.
*At the doctor'**s**.* (anstelle von: *At the doctor'**s** office.*)	Beim Arzt.

Schlage die Seite 52 auf und finde das Genitiv-s im Zusammenhang mit der Ortsangabe.

13. In den Texten des **sechsten Kapitels** (Family matters) sind einige persönliche Fürwörter (Personalpronomen) versteckt. Du kennst sie schon aus navi 5/6, zum Beispiel *you, he, we*.
    - Finde weitere und schreibe alle in eine Liste.
    - Versuche zu erklären, wofür persönliche Fürwörter genutzt werden.
    - Kannst du einige kurze Sätze bilden, in denen persönliche Fürwörter vorkommen? Versuche es.

14. In den Texten des **siebten Kapitels** (What if ...) sind einige Verhältniswörter (Präpositionen) versteckt. Du kennst sie schon aus navi 5/6, zum Beispiel *on, under*.
    - Finde weitere und schreibe sie in eine Liste.
    - Versuche zu erklären, wofür Verhältniswörter genutzt werden.
    - Kannst du einige kurze Sätze bilden, in denen Verhältniswörter vorkommen? Versuche es.

15. Im **achten Kapitel** (United States of America) hast du gelernt, Fragen zu stellen, um bestimmte Informationen zu bekommen. Schaue dir die Fragen auf der Seite 87 noch einmal an.

    - Schreibe die Fragewörter heraus und finde eine deutsche Übersetzung.
    - Welches Fragewort brauchst du, um die unterstrichenen Informationen zu bekommen?

16. Stelle die Fragen nach den unterstrichenen Informationen.

    308 million people live in the United States.

    In 2009 the President of the United States was Barack Obama.

    The President lives in the White House.

17. Arbeite mit einem Partner:
    Schreibt einen der kurzen Texte aus „Plan your journey to the US" ab. Unterstreicht fünf Informationen und überlegt, wie man danach fragt. Schreibt auch die Fragen auf.

18. Im **neunten Kapitel** (Memorial Day and Independence Day) geht es um amerikanische Feiertage.
    Schau dir diese Sätze an.

    a. This is what you have learned.
    b. Since then I have had nightmares.
    c. Paul has asked his grandfather.
    d. Emily has used wrong information.
    e. I have been in the war.
    f. Emily and Paul have made a presentation about Memorial Day.
    g. Since then I have felt ignored.

    - Schreibe die Sätze in dein Heft.
    - Unterstreiche die Verben (Tätigkeitswörter).
    - Was fällt dir auf?
    - Welche Zeitform stellen diese Sätze dar?

19. Schau dir diese Sätze aus dem **zehnten Kapitel** (In the future I will …) an:

Well, I think I'm going to find a job as a waitress.

And I'm going to marry Paul.

I'm going to have two cats.

I'll live in my own house in Bristol.

I think I'll be a popstar.

But maybe he'll be my husband.

- Wird über die Vergangenheit, die Gegenwart oder die Zukunft gesprochen?
- Schreib die Sätze in dein Heft.
- Schau dir die ersten drei Sätze an. Unterstreiche die Wörter, die in allen drei Sätzen vorkommen.
- Schau dir die letzten drei Sätze an. Unterstreiche die Wörter, die in allen drei Sätzen vorkommen.
- Was fällt dir auf?

Kapitel 1
Zeitadverb (unbestimmtes Umstandswort der Zeit)

Mit Zeitadverbien drückt man aus, wie häufig etwas geschieht. Meist handelt es sich um Gewohnheiten oder um Dinge, die man gewöhnlich nicht tut.

She often surfs the internet.

She always reads her e-mail.

She sometimes chats with friends.

She never gives her phone number to strangers.

Das **Zeitadverb** steht immer vor dem **Verb des Satzes**.

Das Verb des Satzes steht häufig in der einfachen Gegenwartsform (simple present) oder in der einfachen Vergangenheitsform (simple past).

Verlaufsform als Satzobjekt (Gerundium)

Was so kompliziert klingt, ist eigentlich ganz einfach: Die Verlaufsform eines Verbs kennst du schon. Sie wird aus der Grundform des Verbs und **-ing** gebildet.

to play ➔ play**ing**
to read ➔ read**ing**
to go ➔ go**ing**
to cook ➔ cook**ing**

Bei Verben, die auf ‚e' enden, fällt das ‚e' weg.

to dan**ce** ➔ dan**cing**
to wri**te** ➔ wri**ting**

Bei Verben, die auf ‚**l**', ‚**m**', ‚**n**', ‚**p**', ‚**s**' oder ‚**t**' enden, verdoppelt sich der letzte Buchstabe.

to cha**t** ➔ chat**ting**
to sto**p** ➔ stop**ping**
to trave**l** ➔ travel**ling**
to ru**n** ➔ run**ning**

like, don't like, hate, love

Nach diesen Verben steht das, was man mag oder nicht mag, manchmal in der Verlaufsform (-ing-Form) als Satzobjekt.

*I **like** playing football.*
*I **don't like** going fishing.*
*I **love** surfing the internet.*
*I **hate** writing letters.*

Die Verlaufsform ist dabei das Objekt des Satzes (Satzergänzung) und wird als Hauptwort betrachtet (Wen oder was mag man?).

Kapitel 2
Steigerung von Adjektiven

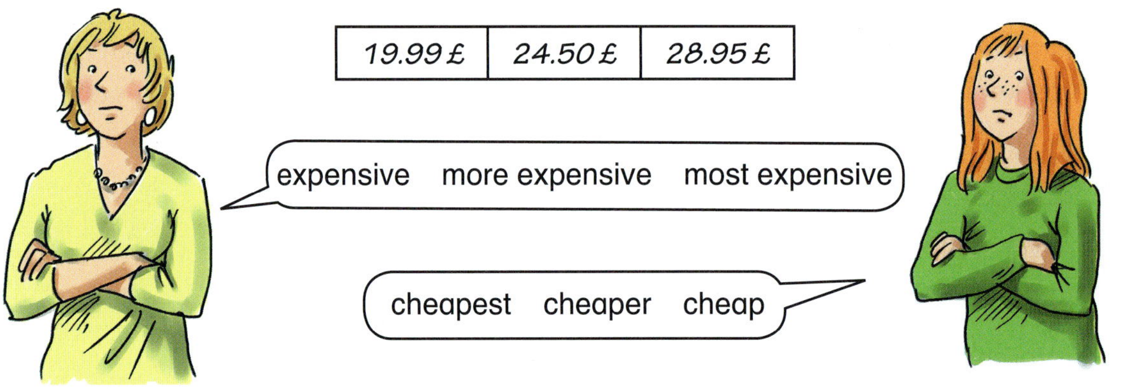

Alle kurzen Eigenschaftswörter (Adjektive) werden mit **-er, -est** gesteigert. Es sind meist einsilbige und kurze zweisilbige Wörter mit der Endung *-le, -er, -ow, -y*.

fast, faster, fastest	(schnell, schneller, (am) schnellsten)
tall, taller, tallest	(groß, größer, (am) größten)
clever, cleverer, cleverest	(klug, klüger, (am) klügsten)
narrow, narrower, narrowest	(eng, enger, (am) engsten)

Besonderheiten bei der Schreibung:

Endung mit -y	eas**y**, eas**i**er, eas**i**est pretty, prettier, prettiest	Das y am Ende des Wortes wird zum i bei der Steigerung.
Adjektive mit kurzem Vokal	bi**g**, bi**gg**er, bi**gg**est sad, sadder, saddest	Wenn der Selbstlaut (Vokal) kurz ist, wird der Mitlaut (Konsonant) danach bei der Steigerung verdoppelt.
Endung mit -e	fin**e**, finer, finest late, later, latest	Das -e am Ende des Wortes fällt bei der Steigerung weg.
Endung mit -le	simp**le**, simpler, simplest	Das -e am Ende des Wortes fällt bei der Steigerung weg.

Es gibt ein paar unregelmäßige Steigerungen:
good, better, best
bad, worse, worst
little, less, least
much/many, more, most

Alle langen Wörter mit mehr als zwei Silben werden mit **more**, **most** gesteigert.

beautiful, more beautiful, most beautiful
difficult, more difficult, most difficult
wonderful, more wonderful, most wonderful
elegant, more elegant, most elegant

Kapitel 3
Die Vergleichsform von Adjektiven

Wenn du Dinge oder Menschen miteinander vergleichen möchtest, musst du etwas über die **Steigerung von Adjektiven** wissen (siehe Kapitel 2). Genauso wie im Deutschen gibt es drei Formen: die Grundform, die Vergleichsform und den Superlativ.

Ein Beispiel

	Grundform	Vergleichsform	Superlativ
auf Deutsch	schnell	schnell**er**	am schnell**sten**
auf Englisch	fast	fast**er**	the fast**est**

Wenn du nun Menschen oder Dinge miteinander vergleichen möchtest, benutzt du die zweite Form, die Vergleichsform in Verbindung mit **than**:

Lukas is taller than Mona. (Lukas ist größer als Mona.)
Jim is younger than John. (Jim ist jünger als John.)
Math is more difficult than English. (Mathe ist schwieriger als Englisch.)

Wenn du Menschen oder Dinge miteinander vergleichst und ausdrücken möchtest, wer der/die beste oder schnellste etc. ist, dann benutzt du die dritte Form, den Superlativ:

Jacky ist the sportiest of all of them. (Jacky ist die sportlichste von allen.)
Terry is the shortest. (Terry ist der Kleinste.)
Kathy is the most elegant person. (Kathy ist die eleganteste Person.)

Wenn du Menschen oder Dinge miteinander vergleichst und feststellst, dass sie gleich sind, dann drückst du dies so aus:

Merke

as + Adjektiv + **as**

Mary is **as** beautiful **as** Celin. (Mary ist **so** schön **wie** Celin.)
Tom is **as** funny **as** Bob. (Tom ist **so** lustig **wie** Bob.)
Kim is **as** tall **as** Thomas. (Kim ist **so** groß **wie** Thomas.)

Die Befehlsform

Wenn du etwas bestimmen oder befehlen möchtest, brauchst du den so genannten Imperativ (Befehlsform). Du hast die Befehlsform bereits in navi 7/8 kennengelernt. Dafür benutzt du die Grundform eines Verbs:

Sit down!	(Setz dich hin!)
Play with me!	(Spiel mit mir!)
Read the text!	(Lies den Text!)
Listen to me!	(Hör mir zu!)
Kiss me!	(Küss mich!)

Wenn du etwas nicht möchtest, stellst du die Verneinung vor das Verb:

Don't sit down!	(Setz dich nicht hin!)
Don't play that game!	(Spiele nicht das Spiel!)
Don't read the text!	(Lies nicht den Text!)
Don't listen to him!	(Hör nicht auf ihn!)
Don't kiss me!	(Küss mich nicht!)

Kapitel 4
Bindewörter

Mit Bindewörtern (Konjunktionen) kannst du Sätze miteinander verbinden. Es gibt viele Bindewörter. Hier lernst du folgende Bindewörter kennen:

- or — oder
- and — und
- but — aber
- because — weil

Outfit A

Outfit B

Do you like outfit A **or** do you like outfit B?
Magst du Outfit A **oder** magst du Outfit B?

I like outfit A **because** yellow is my favourite colour.
Ich mag Outfit A, **weil** gelb meine Lieblingsfarbe ist.

I like outfit B **but** without the scarf.
Ich mag Outfit B, **aber** ohne den Schal.

I like outfit A **and** I would like to go out with the boy.
Ich mag Outfit A **und** würde mit dem Jungen gern ausgehen.

Kapitel 5
Der Besitzfall

Wenn du deutlich machen möchtest, dass jemandem etwas gehört oder jemand einer Gruppe angehört, wendest du den Besitzfall (s-Genitiv) an:

- Wenn das Hauptwort in der Einzahl steht, wird ein Apostroph mit s (**'s**) angehängt:

*John**'s** band is wellknown.*	Johns Band ist bekannt.
*Mona**'s** brother is sixteen.*	Monas Bruder ist sechzehn.

- Wenn das Hauptwort in der Mehrzahl steht, wird nur ein Apostroph (**'**) angehängt:

*The boys**'** bags got stolen.*	Die Taschen der Jungs wurden geklaut.
*The girls**'** hobby is skating.*	Das Hobby der Mädchen ist Skaten.

Wenn die Mehrzahlbildung aber unregelmäßig ist, also nicht auf -s endet, so wird wie bei der Einzahl ein **'s** angehängt:

The children's songs were great. Die Lieder der Kinder waren toll.
Men's clothes are sold out. Die Kleidung der Männer ist ausverkauft.

Wenn das Bezugswort eine Ortsangabe ist, wie zum Beispiel *house, flat* oder *shop*, wird dieses Wort meist weggelassen:

At the painter's (shop). Beim Maler.
At the Newman's (house). Bei den Newmans.
At Rosalie's (hair salon). Bei Rosalies Friseurladen.

Merke Der Besitzfall (s-Genitiv) hat nichts mit der Kurzform von „is" zu tun.

Kapitel 6
Persönliche Fürwörter

In navi 5/6 hast du bereits persönliche Fürwörter (Personalpronomen) kennen gelernt. Wenn du über dich oder andere Personen sprichst, kannst du den Namen der Person immer wieder nennen. Dann aber wiederholst du ständig, und das hört sich oft nicht so gut an. Du kannst daher die Personalpronomen verwenden. Man nennt persönliche Fürwörter auch Personalpronomen.

Zu der Gruppe der Personalpronomen gehören folgende Wörter:

Personalpronomen – Personal pronouns

Englisch	Deutsch
I	ich
you	du
he	er
she	sie
it	es
we	wir
you	ihr (*Gruppe*)/Sie (*Siezform*)
they	sie (*Gruppe*)

Beispiele	
Englisch	**Deutsch**
1. **I** will be home at eight o'clock.	**Ich** werde um acht Uhr zu Hause sein.
2. Is it really **you**?	Bist **du** es wirklich?
3. **He** is very nice.	**Er** ist sehr nett.
4. **She** is very nice, too.	**Sie** ist auch sehr nett.
5. **It** is so cute.	**Es** ist so süß.
6. **We** really have to go.	**Wir** müssen wirklich los.
7. Must **you** really go?	Müsst **Ihr**/Müssen **Sie** wirklich los? (*Wenn von einer Gruppe gesprochen oder eine Person gesiezt wird.*)
8. **They** will be back in a few days.	**Sie** werden in einigen Tagen zurück sein. (*Wenn von einer Gruppe gesprochen wird.*)

Merke Nach dem Satzteil mit dem Personalpronomen fragst du mit dem Fragewort **wer**.

Beispiele:

Paul is my neighbour. He is nice. Paul ist mein Nachbar. Er ist nett.

Frage: Wer ist dein Nachbar? Wer ist nett?

Antwort: Paul ist mein Nachbar. Paul ist nett.

Besitzanzeigende Fürwörter

Wenn du ausdrücken möchtest, wem etwas gehört, wer also etwas besitzt, dann kannst du die besitzanzeigenden Fürwörter (Possessivpronomen) verwenden. Du hast sie bereits in navi 5/6 kennengelernt.

Zu der Gruppe der Possessivpronomen gehören folgende Wörter:

Possessivpronomen – Possessive pronouns

Englisch	Deutsch
my	mein
your	dein
his	sein
her	ihr
its	sein (*sächlich*)
our	unser
your	euer
their	deren

Beispiele	
Englisch	**Deutsch**
1. Is this **my** bag?	Ist dies **meine** Tasche?
2. Is this **your** bag?	Ist dieses **deine** Tasche?
3. That is **his** sister.	Das ist **seine** Schwester.
4. Is that **her** brother?	Ist das **ihr** Bruder?
5. The dog has got a new hut. It likes **its** new home.	Der Hund hat eine neue Hütte. Er mag **sein** neues Heim.
6. It is **our** car.	Es ist **unser** Auto.
7. That is **your** decision.	Das ist **eure** Entscheidung. (*Wenn von einer Gruppe gesprochen wird.*)
8. That is **their** decision.	Das ist **deren** Entscheidung.

Merke Nach dem Satzteil mit dem Possessivpronomen fragst du mit dem Fragewort **wem** (gehört).

Beispiele:

*This is **my** new mobile phone.* Dies ist **mein** neues Handy.

Frage: Wem gehört das neue Handy?

Antwort: Das neue Handy gehört **mir**.

Die Objektpronomen

Wenn du ausdrücken möchtest, mit wem du etwas unternimmst oder mit wem du zum Beispiel auf einem Foto zu sehen bist, kannst du die Objektpronomen verwenden.
Zu der Gruppe der Objektpronomen gehören folgende Wörter:

Objektpronomen – Personal pronouns and determiners

Englisch	**Deutsch**	
Who?	**Wem?**	**Wen?**
me	mir	mich
you*	dir	dich*
him	ihm	ihn
her	ihr	sie
us	uns	uns
you	euch	euch
them	ihnen	sie
you*	Ihnen	Sie*

** Bei dem Objektpronomen **you** unterscheidet man im Deutschen zwischen der **Duzform** und der **Siezform**. Im Englischen wird dieser Unterschied nicht gemacht.*

Beispiele	
Englisch	**Deutsch**
1. What is happening with **me**?	Was passiert mit **mir**?
2. I would like to go to the cinema with **you**.	Ich würde gerne mit **dir** ins Kino gehen.
3. It was nice of **him** to help.	Es war nett von **ihm** zu helfen.

Beispiele	
Englisch	**Deutsch**
4. Was it not great of **her** to be here?	War es nicht großartig von **ihr**, hier zu sein?
5. It will be difficult for **us** to find a taxi.	Es wird schwierig für **uns** sein, ein Taxi zu finden.
6. It must have been a long journey for **you**.	Es muss eine lange Reise für **euch** gewesen sein.
7. Thanks to them **we** made it in time.	Dank **ihnen** haben wir es rechtzeitig geschafft. (*Wenn von einer Gruppe gesprochen wird.*)
8. Thanks to you **we** made it in time.	Dank **Ihnen** haben wir es rechtzeitig geschafft. (*Wenn von einer Person gesprochen wird, die gesiezt wird.*)

Merke Nach dem Satzteil mit dem Objektpronomen fragst du mit **wem** oder **was** (Dativ) oder **wen** oder **was** (Akkusativ).

Beispiele:

That is Paul with ***me*** *in the photo.* Das ist Paul mit **mir** auf dem Foto.

Frage: Mit **wem** ist Paul auf dem Foto?

Antwort: Mit **mir** (ist Paul auf dem Foto).

Kapitel 7
Verhältniswörter

Wenn du ausdrücken möchtest, wo sich eine Person oder ein Gegenstand befindet, benutzt du Verhältniswörter (Präpositionen). Du hast sie bereits in navi 5/6 kennen gelernt. Sie beschreiben, in welchem **Verhältnis** sich Personen oder Gegenstände zueinander befinden. Dabei unterscheidet man zwischen der Gruppe der **Ortspräpositionen** und der Gruppe der **Richtungspräpositionen**:

Ortspräpositionen

Englisch	**Deutsch**
at	an/bei
on	auf
behind	hinter
in	in
above	über
under	unter
in front of/before (zeitlich)*	vor*
between	zwischen
opposite	gegenüber
beside/next to	neben

** Bei der Präposition **in front of/before** unterscheidet man zwischen **Ortsangaben** und **Zeitangaben**.*

*Für **Ortsangaben:*** ***in front of***

*Für **Zeitangaben:*** ***before***

Beispiele	
Englisch	**Deutsch**
1. The car is **in front** of the shop.	Das Auto ist **vor** dem Geschäft.
2. It happened shortly **before** the shop opened.	Es passierte kurz **bevor** das Geschäft öffnete.
3. The lamp shop lies **opposite** the restaurant.	Das Lampengeschäft liegt **gegenüber** dem Restaurant.
4. Paul sits **between** Cem and Emily.	Paul sitzt **neben** Cem und Emily.
5. The pencil is **on** the desk.	Der Bleistift ist **auf** dem Schreibtisch.

Richtungspräpositionen

Englisch	Deutsch
into	in …/nach … hinein
onto	auf … herauf
out of	aus … heraus
towards	auf … zu
around	um … herum
after	hinter … her
across/over*	herüber*
up	hoch/hinauf
down	herunter
along	entlang
through	durch

** Bei der Präposition **across/over** gibt es keinen besonderen Unterschied.*

Beispiele	
Englisch	**Deutsch**
1. The person drives the car **into** the garage.	Die Person fährt das Auto **in** die Garage (**hinein**).
2. The shop assistant takes the goods **of** the shelf.	Der Verkäufer nimmt die Ware **aus** dem Regal (**heraus**).
3. The police drive **around** the corner.	Die Polizei fährt um die Ecke (**herum**).
4. The ball flies **through** the window.	Der Ball fliegt **durch** das Fenster.
5. The plain flies **across/over** the ocean.	Das Flugzeug fliegt **über** den Ozean (**herüber**).

Die Präposition steht **hinter dem Verb/Hilfsverb**. Das ist im Deutschen auch so.

Kapitel 8
Wh-Fragen

Bisher hast du in erster Linie Entscheidungsfragen kennen gelernt, die man mit „ja“ oder „nein“ beantworten kann. Oft möchte man aber auch **nach einer bestimmten Information fragen**. Dann benutzt man die **„Wh-Fragen“**.

Wh-Fragen sind Fragen, die ein Fragewort am Anfang haben. Sie sind dir auch schon in navi 5/6 begegnet.

Folgende Fragewörter werden häufig benutzt:

Who?	Wer?
Where?	Wo?
What?	Was?
When?	Wann?
How much? How many?	Wie viel(e)?

Pass bei der Übersetzung von “who” und “where” auf. Die englischen Worte sind sozusagen “umgekehrt” zu den deutschen Übersetzungen.

Merke Fragewörter stehen immer am Anfang einer Frage.

Who *is the President of the United States?*
Where *is Washington?*
What *is the Statue of Liberty?*
When *do we meet?*
How *many people live in the United States?*
How *much money have you got?*

Kapitel 9
Die vollendete Gegenwart

Wenn du über Vorgänge sprechen möchtest, die in der Vergangenheit passiert sind, deren Ergebnis sich aber noch auf die Gegenwart auswirkt, verwendest du die vollendete Gegenwart (das Perfekt). Im Englischen heißt die Zeitform *present perfect*.

Zum Beispiel:

I have played football. My shirt is dirty. Ich habe Fußball gespielt. Mein Shirt ist dreckig.

I have played football.	Ich habe Fußball gespielt.
You have played football.	Du hast Fußball gespielt.
He has played football.	Er hat Fußball gespielt.
She has played football.	Sie hat Fußball gespielt.
It has rained.	Es hat geregnet.
We have played football.	Wir haben Fußball gespielt.
You have played football.	Ihr habt Fußball gespielt.
They have played football.	Sie haben Fußball gespielt.

So wird die vollendete Gegenwart bei regelmäßigen Verben gebildet:

Merke

+ have/has + Grundform mit der Endung -ed

+ have not/has not + Grundform mit der Endung -ed

+ haven't/hasn't + Grundform mit der Endung -ed

Bei unregelmäßigen Verben wird anstelle der Grundform und der Endung -ed das Partizip Perfekt gewählt. Diese Verben musst du lernen. Schaue dir die Liste der unregelmäßigen Verben auf den Seiten 140 und 141 an.

Kapitel 10
Die Zukunft

Wenn du darüber sprechen möchtest, was in der Zukunft passieren wird, kannst du im Englischen das *will-future* oder das *going to-future* verwenden.

Will-Future

Du benutzt das *will-future*, um eine **Vorhersage** auszudrücken. Sie ist meist mit einer Zeitangabe verbunden.

I will swim tomorrow. I'll swim tomorrow.	Ich werde morgen schwimmen.
You will swim tomorrow. You'll swim tomorrow.	Du wirst morgen schwimmen.
He will swim tomorrow. He'll swim tomorrow.	Er wird morgen schwimmen.
She will swim tomorrow. She'll swim tomorrow.	Sie wird morgen schwimmen.
We will swim tomorrow. We'll swim tomorrow.	Wir werden morgen schwimmen.
You will swim tomorrow. You'll swim tomorrow.	Ihr werdet morgen schwimmen.
They will swim tomorrow. They'll swim tomorrow.	Sie werden morgen schwimmen.

So wird das will-future gebildet:

Merke

+ will + Grundform des Verbs

+ 'll + Grundform des Verbs

+ will not + Grundform des Verbs

+ won't + Grundform des Verbs

I will bedeutet nicht *ich will,* sondern *ich werde*

Going to-future

Du benutzt das going to-future, um eine **Absicht** auszudrücken.

I am going to run. I'm going to run.	Ich habe vor zu rennen.
You are going to run. You're going to run.	Du hast vor zu rennen.
He is going to run. He's going to run.	Er hat vor zu rennen.
She is going to run. She's going to run.	Sie hat vor zu rennen.
It is going to run. It's going to run.	Es hat vor zu rennen.
We are going to run. We're going to run.	Wir haben vor zu rennen.
You are going to run. You're going to run.	Ihr habt vor zu rennen.
They are going to run. They're going to run.	Sie haben vor zu rennen.

So wird das going to-future gebildet:

Merke

+ am/are/is + going to + Grundform des Verbs

+ 'm/'re/'s + going to + Grundform des Verbs

+ am/are/is + not + going to + Grundform des Verbs

+ 'm not/aren't/isn't + going to + Grundform des Verbs

Unregelmäßige Verben

	Grundform	Vergangenheit	Partizip	Deutsch
to	babysit	babysat	babysat	babysitten
to	be	was/were	been	sein
to	beat	beat	beaten	schlagen
to	become	became	become	werden
to	begin	began	begun	anfangen
to	bet	bet	bet	wetten
to	blow	blew	blown	blasen
to	break	broke	broken	zerbrechen
to	bring	brought	brought	bringen
to	buy	bought	bought	kaufen
to	build	built	built	bauen
to	burn	burnt	burnt	verbrennen
to	buy	bought	bought	kaufen
to	catch	caught	caught	fangen
to	choose	chose	chosen	aussuchen, auswählen
to	come	came	come	kommen
to	do	did	done	tun
to	draw	drew	drawn	zeichnen
to	drink	drank	drunk	trinken
to	drive	drove	driven	fahren
to	eat	ate	eaten	essen
to	fall in love	fell in love	fallen in love	sich verlieben
to	feed	fed	fed	füttern
to	feel	felt	felt	fühlen
to	fight	fought	fought	kämpfen
to	find	found	found	finden
to	fly	flew	flown	fliegen
to	forget	forgot	forgotten	vergessen
to	freeze	froze	frozen	frieren
to	get	got	got	bekommen
to	give	gave	given	geben
to	go	went	gone	gehen
to	grow	grew	grown	wachsen

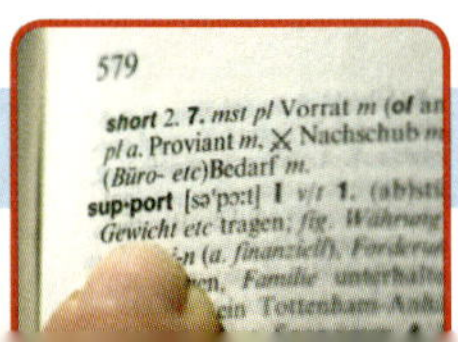

	Grundform	Vergangenheit	Partizip	Deutsch
to	hang	hung	hung	hängen
to	have	had	had	haben
to	hit	hit	hit	treffen, schlagen
to	keep	kept	kept	behalten
to	know	knew	known	wissen
to	leave	left	left	verlassen, lassen
to	lie	lay	lain	liegen
to	lose	lost	lost	verlieren
to	make	made	made	machen
to	mean	meant	meant	bedeuten
to	meet	met	met	treffen
to	pay	paid	paid	zahlen, bezahlen
to	read	read	read	lesen, vorlesen
to	ring	rang	rung	klingeln, läuten
to	run	ran	run	rennen
to	say	said	said	sagen
to	see	saw	seen	sehen, schauen
to	sell	sold	sold	verkaufen
to	show	showed	shown	zeigen
to	sing	sang	sung	singen
to	sit	sat	sat	sitzen
to	sleep	slept	slept	schlafen
to	speak	spoke	spoken	sprechen
to	spend	spent	spent	verbringen, ausgeben
to	stand	stood	stood	stehen
to	swim	swam	swum	schwimmen
to	take	took	taken	nehmen
to	teach	taught	taught	unterrichten
to	tell	told	told	erzählen
to	think	thought	thought	denken
to	throw	threw	thrown	werfen
to	wear	wore	worn	tragen
to	win	won	won	gewinnen
to	write	wrote	written	schreiben

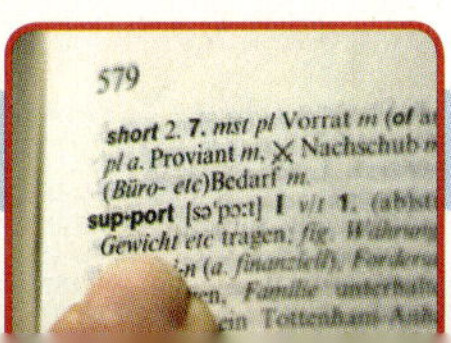

Zahlwörter

1	one
2	two
3	three
4	four
5	five
6	six
7	seven
8	eight
9	nine
10	ten
11	eleven
12	twelve
13	thirteen
14	fourteen
15	fifteen
16	sixteen
17	seventeen
18	eighteen
19	nineteen
20	twenty
21	twenty-one
22	twenty-two
23	twenty-three
...	
30	thirty
31	thirty-one
32	thirty-two
...	
40	forty
50	fifty
60	sixty
70	seventy
80	eighty
90	ninety
100	one hundred
101	one hundred and one
110	one hundred (and) ten
120	one hundred (and) twenty
121	one hundred (and) twenty-one
200	two hundred

1st	(the) first
2nd	(the) second
3rd	(the) third
4th	(the) fourth
5th	(the) fifth
6th	(the) sixth
7th	(the) seventh
8th	(the) eighth
9th	(the) ninth
10th	(the) tenth
11th	(the) eleventh
12th	(the) twelfth
13th	(the) thirteenth
14th	(the) fourteenth
15th	(the) fifteenth
16th	(the) sixteenth
17th	(the) seventeenth
18th	(the) eighteenth
19th	(the) nineteenth
20th	(the) twentieth
21st	(the) twenty-first
22nd	(the) twenty-second
23rd	(the) twenty-third
24th	(the) twenty-fourth
...	
30th	(the) thirtieth
31st	(the) thirty-first
32nd	(the) thirty-second
33rd	(the) thirty-third
34th	(the) thirty-fourth
...	

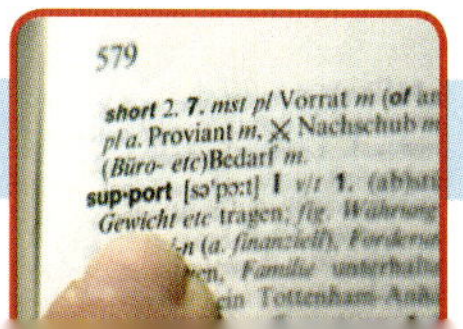

Vocabulary

A

	a	ein, eine
	a long time ago	lange her
	a lot (of)	viel, viele
an	abbreviation	eine Abkürzung
	about	um, über
	above	oben
an	abuse	ein Missbrauch
	absolutely	absolut
to	accentuate	betonen, hervorheben
to	accept	entgegennehmen, akzeptieren
an	accessoire	ein Accessoire
an	accident	ein Unfall
	accidentally	ausversehen
an	account number	eine Kontonummer
	across	quer hinüber
to	act	spielen
an	activity	eine Aktivität
an	ad	eine Anzeige (Kurzform)
to	add	hinzufügen
an	address	eine Adresse
	addresses	Adressen
an	adjective	ein Adjektiv
an	adult	ein Erwachsener
an	advertisement	eine Anzeige
an	advice	ein Ratschlag
to	advise	beraten
	afraid	ängstlich, besorgt
	after	nach
an	afternoon	ein Nachmittag
	again	wieder, noch einmal
the	age	das Alter
an	agency	eine Agentur
	aggressive	aggressiv
to	agree	zustimmen, einwilligen
an	agreement	eine Zustimmung
	ahead	vor
an	airport	ein Flughafen
an	aisle seat	ein Platz am Gang
an	alien	ein Außerirdischer
	all	alle
	all together	alle zusammen
	almost	fast
	along – sing along, read along	mit – mitsingen, mitlesen
	already	bereits
	always	immer
	a.m.	morgens, am Vormittag (bei Uhrzeiten)
an	ambulance	ein Krankenwagen
	America	Amerika
an	American	eine Amerikanerin, ein Amerikaner
an	amount	eine Menge
	and	und
	and so on	und so weiter
	angry, angrier, the angriest	wütend, wütender, am wütesten
an	animal	ein Tier
an	animal shelter	ein Tierheim
an	announcement	eine Durchsage
	anonymous	anonym
an	answer	eine Antwort
to	answer	antworten
	any	irgendeiner, irgendeine, irgendetwas
	anybody	irgendjemand
an	apartment (AE[1])	eine Wohnung
an	applicant	ein Bewerber, eine Bewerberin
an	application	eine Bewerbung

[1] AE = amerikanisches Englisch

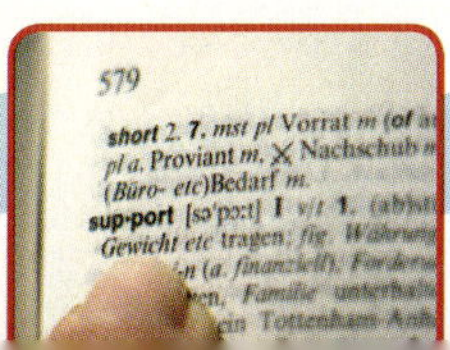

to	apply	sich bewerben
an	apron	eine Schürze
	are	sind
an	area	eine Gegend
an	argument	ein Argument
	around the corner	um die Ecke
to	arrange	arrangieren
	arrival	Ankunft
to	arrive	ankommen
an	artist	ein Künstler, eine Künstlerin
	as	als
to	ask	fragen
	at	an, bei
	at that time	damals
	at all	überhaupt
	at home	zu Hause
	at least	wenigstens
to	attack	angreifen
to	attract	anlocken, reizen, anziehen
an	aunt	eine Tante
	autumn	Herbst
to	avoid	verhindern, vermeiden

B

to	babysit	babysitten
	back	zurück
	bad weather	schlechtes Wetter
a	bag	eine Tasche
	baggage	Gepäck
	baggy pants	weite, tiefsitzende Hose
a	baker	ein Bäcker, eine Bäckerin
a	bakery	eine Bäckerei
a	bank	eine Bank (Geldinstitut)
a	bank code	eine Bankleitzahl (BLZ)
a	banner	ein Banner, eine Fahne
a	bar (AE)	eine Bar, Kneipe
a	bar chart	ein Balken-diagramm
a	barbecue	eine Grillparty
a	barkeeper	ein Barkeeper, eine Barkeeperin
a	bathroom	ein Badezimmer
a	batik fabric	ein Batikstoff
to	be, was/were	sein
to	be attracted by someone	von jemandem angezogen sein
to	be bullied	geärgert werden, schikaniert werden
to	be delayed	verspätet sein
to	be excited	aufgeregt sein
to	be famous for sth.	für etw. berühmt sein
to	be impressed	beeindruckt sein
to	be in love	verliebt sein
to	be in love with someone	jemanden lieben
to	be in touch with	Kontakt haben
to	be late	zu spät sein
to	be less expensive	billiger sein
to	be lucky	Glück haben
to	be popular	beliebt sein
to	be present	dabei sein
to	be ready	fertig sein
to	be right	recht haben
a	beach	ein Strand
to	beam sth/s.o.	etw./jmd. beamen
a	beamer	ein Beamer
a	beard	ein Bart
	beautiful, more beautiful, the most beautiful	schön, schöner, am schönsten
	because	weil
to	become	werden
	before	vorher
a	beginning	ein Anfang
	behind	hinter

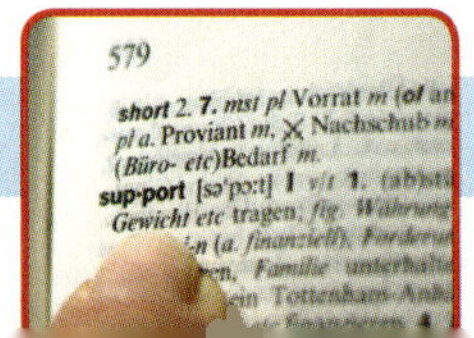

a	bell	eine Klingel, eine Glocke
to	belong to	zu … gehören
a	belt	ein Gürtel
a	bench	eine Sitzbank
	benches	Sitzbänke
the	best	beste, bester, bestes
to	bet	wetten
	between	zwischen
	big	groß, großer, große, großes
a	big/small building	ein großes/kleines Gebäude
	bigger	größer
a	bike	ein Fahrrad
a	bike tour	eine Fahrradtour
a	bill	eine Rechnung
a	birthday	ein Geburtstag
	black	schwarz
	blind	blind
a	blind date	eine Verabredung, bei der sich die Personen noch nie vorher gesehen haben
	blond	blond
a	blouse	eine Bluse
to	blow to pieces	in Stücke sprengen
to	blow-dry	föhnen
	blue	blau
a	board	eine Tafel
to	board	einsteigen (in eine Flugzeug)
a	board game	ein Brettspiel
a	boarding card	eine Bordkarte
a	boarding school	ein Internat
a	bodice	ein Korsett
a	book	ein Buch
to	book	buchen
a	boot	ein Kofferaum
a	boot (AE)	ein Stiefel
a	border	eine Grenze

	bored	gelangweilt
	boring	langweilig
a	boss	ein Chef, eine Chefin
	both	beide
the	bottom	der Grund
the	bottom half	die untere Hälfte
a	box	ein Kasten, ein Kästchen
a	boy	ein Junge
a	boyfriend	ein (fester) Freund
a	brand	eine Marke
a	bread	ein Brot
a	bricklayer	ein Maurer, eine Maurerin
a	bridge	eine Brücke
to	bring, brought	bringen
the	British	die Briten
a	brochure	eine Broschüre
a	brooch	eine Brosche
	brown	braun
	brunette	brünett
to	brush	bürsten
to	brush the teeth	die Zähne putzen
a	buddy	ein Kumpel
to	build, built, built	bauen
a	building	ein Gebäude
	biscuits	Kekse
a	bullet point	ein Aufzählungs-zeichen
a	bureau de change	Geldwechsel
a	burn	eine Verbrennung
to	burn	verbrennen
a	bus driver	eine Busfahrerin, ein Busfahrer
a	bus station	eine Bushaltestelle
a	bus stop	eine Bushaltestelle
	business look	aussehen wie ein Geschäftsmann
	busy	beschäftigt
	but	aber
a	butterfly	ein Schmetterling

a	button	Knopf, Schaltfläche im Programm
to	buy	kaufen
	by	hier: durch

C

	C-ya = See you	Bis später (Verabschiedung).
a	cab (AE)	ein Taxi
a	café	ein Café
a	cage	ein Käfig
	California	Kalifornien
a	call	ein Anruf
to	call	anrufen
	called	genannt
	can	können
	Canada	Kanada
a	candle-light-dinner	ein Kerzenschein-Essen
	candy (AE)	Süßigkeiten
a	canyon	eine Schlucht
a	cap	eine Mütze, eine Kappe
a	capital	eine Hauptstadt
a	car	ein Auto
to	care about	sich kümmern um
	careful	vorsichtig
a	carer	ein Erziehungsbe-rechtiger
	carrot pants	Karrottenhose
to	carve	schnitzen
a	cash machine	ein Geldautomat
a	cashier	ein Kassierer, eine Kassiererin
a	casino	ein Kasino
	casual	lässig, sportlich
a	cat	eine Katze
a	catalogue	ein Katalog
to	catch up with s.o	jmd. einholen
to	celebrate	feiern

a	chance	eine Chance
a	change	eine Veränderung
to	change	verändern, wechseln, tauschen
a	chart	ein Schaubild
a	chat	ein Chat, eine Plauderei
to	chat	plaudern, miteinander reden
a	chat room	ein virtueller Raum im Internet, in dem miteinander schrift-lich kommuniziert wird
	cheap, cheaper, the cheapest	billig, billiger, am billigsten
to	check	überprüfen
	check-in	einchecken
a	check-in desk	Schalter zum Einchecken
	checked	kariert
	cheers	Prosit! (auch Ver-abschiedungsgruß)
a	child,	ein Kind,
the	children	die Kinder
a	chimney sweeper	ein Schornstein-feger
	chips	Pommes Frites
a	choice	Auswahl, Wahl
to	choose	aussuchen, auswählen
	chops	Koteletten
a	Christian name	ein Vorname
a	cinema	ein Kino
to	circle	einkreisen
a	circular chart	ein Kreisdiagramm
a	Citizens Registration Office	ein Einwohner-meldeamt
a	city	eine Großstadt
a	city centre	ein Stadtzentrum
a	city map	ein Stadtplan
a	class	eine Klasse

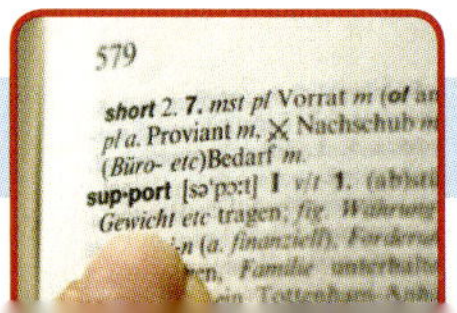

to	clean	sauber machen
to	click on	auf … klicken (mit der Maus)
a	client	eine Kundin, ein Kunde
	close	nahe
	clothes	Kleidung
	cloudy	bewölkt
a	club	ein Club
a	coat	ein Mantel
a	cock	ein Hahn
a	coffee bar	ein Cafe
a	collar	ein Kragen
a	colleague	ein Kollege, eine Kollegin
to	collect	sammeln
a	colour	eine Farbe
to	colour	bunt anmalen
a	column	eine Spalte (Tabelle), Säule
a	comb	ein Kamm
to	comb	kämmen
to	come	kommen
to	come around	vorbeikommen
to	come back	zurückkommen
	comfortable	gemütlich
	common	geläufig, häufig, üblich
to	communicate	kommuizieren
	communication	Kommunikation
a	community college	eine Volkshochschule
to	compare	etw. vergleichen
a	comparison	ein Vergleich
	complete	vollständig
to	complete	vervollständigen, ausfüllen
	completely	komplett
	complicated	kompliziert
a	complication	eine Komplikation
to	compress	verdichten, zusammenpressen

a	computer	ein Computer
	computer hardware	Computerzubehör
a	conception	eine Konzeption, eine Planung
a	concert	ein Konzert
	conditioner	Spülung
	congratulations	Glückwünsche
the	cons	die Gegenargumente
a	constellation	eine Zusammenstellung
a	contact	ein Kontakt
to	contain	enthalten
to	continue	weitermachen
a	contract	ein Vertrag
a	conversation	ein Gespräch
a	cook	ein Koch, eine Köchin
to	cook	kochen
	cookies (AE)	Kekse
	cool	cool, kühl
	correct	richtig
	could	könnten
to	count	zählen
to	count on something, someone	auf etwas oder jemanden zählen
a	country	ein Land
	countryside	(auf dem) Land
a	course	ein Kurs
a	cousin	ein Cousin, eine Cousine
	cousins	Cousins, Cousinen
a	craftsman	ein Handwerker, eine Handwerkerin
	crazy	verrückt
to	create	erschaffen, aufbauen
	creative	kreativ
	creme	Creme
	cricket	Kricket, ein besonderes Ballspiel

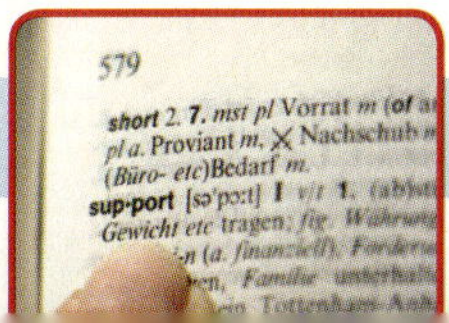

a	criterium	ein Kriterium
the	criteria	die Kriterien
a	cross	ein Kreuz
	crosses	Kreuze
to	cross	überqueren
to	cross out	durchstreichen
a	cry	ein Schrei, ein Ausruf
	cries	Schreie, Ausrufe
to	cry	weinen, schreien, ausrufen
	curly	gelockt
	currency	Währung
	current	jetziger, jetzige, jetziges
a	Curriculum Vitae	ein Lebenslauf

D

a	dad	ein Vater
	dads	Väter
	dangerous	gefährlich
	dark	dunkel
	dark (green)	dunkel (grün)
	data	Daten
a	date	eine Verabredung
to	date	sich verabreden
a	date of birth, birth-day	ein Geburtstag
a	dating agency	eine Verkupplungs-agentur
a	dating system	eine offizielle Verkupplungs-organisation
a	daughter	eine Tochter
a	day	ein Tag
a	daypack	Tagesrucksack
	dear	liebe, lieber (Anrede in einem Brief)
	Dear Sir or Madam	Sehr geehrte Damen und Herren
a	death	ein Tod
to	decide	sich entscheiden
a	decision	eine Entscheidung
a	deck	ein Schiffsdeck
to	declare	verkünden, erklären
	deep	tief
a	defeat	eine Niederlage
to	defeat	schlagen, besiegen
to	deliver	ausliefern, vorbei bringen
to	deliver newspapers	Zeitungen austragen
to	depart	abfliegen, abfahren
	departure	Abflug, Abfahrt
to	describe	beschreiben
a	description	eine Beschreibung
a	desert	Wüste
a	destination	ein Ziel
to	destroy	zerstören
to	develop	entwickeln
a	dialogue	ein Dialog
a	dictionary	ein Wörterbuch
a	die/dice (pl.)	(ein) Würfel
to	die	sterben
	different	anders, unterschiedlich, verschieden
a	diner	ein typisches amerikanisches günstiges Restaurant
the	dirt	Dreck, Schmutz
	dirty	dreckig, schmutzig
a	disabled toilet	Behindertentoilette
to	disagree	nicht zustimmen
to	discuss	diskutieren
a	discussion	eine Diskussion
a	disease	eine Erkrankung
to	dislike	nicht mögen
the	dislikes	Dinge, die man nicht mag

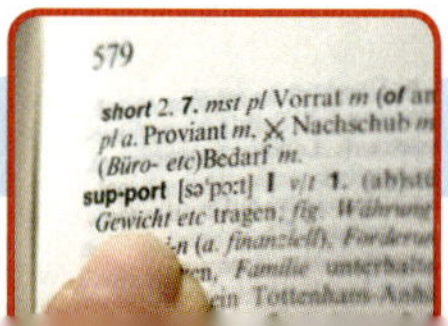

a	divorce	eine Scheidung
to	divorce	sich scheiden lassen
to	do	tun
to	do sports	Sport machen
a	doctor	ein Arzt, eine Ärztin
a	dog	ein Hund
a	donkey	ein Esel
the	donts	Dinge, die nicht in Ordnung sind
the	dos	Dinge, die in Ordnung sind
to	double-click	doppelt mit der Maus klicken
to	draw	zeichnen
a	dream	ein Traum
to	dream of	träumen von
a	dress	ein Kleid
to	drink	trinken
to	drip	tropfen
to	drive	fahren
	due to	wegen
	during	während

E

an	e-mail	eine E-mail
to	e-mail	eine E-Mail schreiben
an	e-mail address	E-Mail-Adresse
	each	jeder, jede, jedes
	each other	einander, gegenseitig
	each time	jedes Mal
	early	früh
to	earn	verdienen
an	earning	Verdienst
	earrings	Ohrringe
	easy, easier, the easiest	leicht, leichter, am leichtesten
to	eat	essen
	Egyptian	ägyptisch
	either … or …	entweder … oder
	neither … nor …	weder … noch …
an	elephant	ein Elefant
an	elevator (AE)	ein Fahrstuhl
	eleven	elf
	embarassing	peinlich
an	emergency	ein Notfall
to	employ	(in ein Arbeitsverhältnis) einstellen
an	employee	ein Angestellter, eine Angestellte
an	employment	ein Arbeitsverhältnis
	empty	leer
an	enemy (pl. enemies)	ein Feind, Feinde
	England	England
	English	englisch, englische, englisches
to	enjoy	genießen, Spaß haben
	enough	genug
	entertaining	unterhaltsam
	erect (hair)	aufgestellte (Haare)
to	erupt	ausbrechen
	even	sogar
	even though	obwohl
an	evening	ein Abend
an	event	ein Ereignis
	every	jeder, jede, jedes
	everyone	jede, jeder
	ex	Ex-… (Mann, Frau, Freund, Freundin)
	exciting	aufregend
an	excuse	eine Entschuldigung
	Excuse me, please.	Entschuldige, bitte.
an	exercise book	ein Übungsheft
	expensive, more expensive, the most expensive	teuer, teurer, am teuersten
an	experience	eine Erfahrung

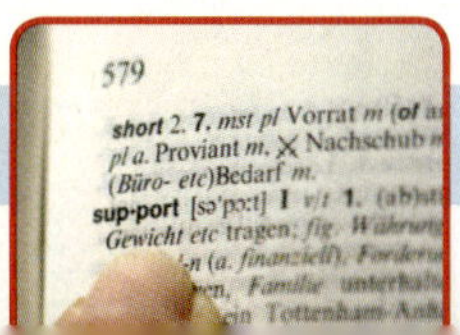

to	experience	erfahren
to	explain	erklären
a	explanation	eine Erklärung
	e**X**tra **L**arge	Größe **XL**
an	eye	ein Auge
	eye shadow	ein Lidschatten
an	eye-contact	ein Augenkontakt
the	eye-lashes	die Augenwimpern

F

a	face	ein Gesicht
a	fact	eine Tatsache
a	factory	eine Fabrik
a	factory worker	ein Fabrikarbeiter, eine Fabrikarbeiterin
a	fair	ein Jahrmarkt
	fall (AE)	Herbst
to	fall in love	sich verlieben
	false	unwahr, falsch
	fame	Berühmtheit
a	family (pl. families)	eine Familie (Familien)
a	family situation	eine Familiensituation
a	family tree	ein Familienstammbaum
	famous	berühmt
	fancy	schick
	fashion	Mode
a	fashion feature	ein Modemerkmal
	fashionable	modisch, schick
	fast, faster, the fastest	schnell, schneller, am schnellsten
a	father	ein Vater
a	fault	ein Fehler
	favourite	Lieblings-
to	feed	füttern
to	feel	fühlen
a	feeling	ein Gefühl
a	female	eine weibliche Person
a	fever	ein Fieber
	fifteen	fünfzehn
	fifty	fünfzig
a	fight	ein Kampf
to	fight	kämpfen
the	figure	die Figur
a	file	eine Datei
to	fill	füllen
to	fill in	ausfüllen
a	film studio	ein Filmstudio
	finally	schließlich
	finally	zum Schluss, letztendlich
to	find, found, found	finden
to	find out	herausfinden
a	fire brigade	eine Feuerwehr
a	firefighter	ein Feuerwehrmann, eine Feuerwehrfrau
	fireworks	ein Feuerwerk
	first	erster, erste, erstes, ersten, zuerst
	five	fünf
a	flag	eine Flagge, eine Fahne
a	flannel shirt	ein Flanellhemd
	flared trousers	eine Schlaghose
	flat	flach
a	flat	eine Wohnung
	flexible	flexibel
a	flight	ein Flug
a	flirt	ein Flirt
a	floor	ein Fußboden, eine Etage, ein Stockwerk
a	floral design	ein Blumenmuster
to	flow	fließen
a	flower	eine Blume
to	fly, flew, flown	fliegen
the	focus	der Fokus

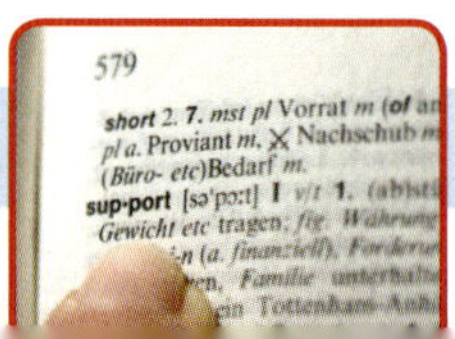

	foggy	neblig
to	fold down	herunterklappen
to	fold up	hochklappen
the	following	die folgenden
	football	Fußball
a	football star	ein Fußballstar
	for	für
	for example	zum Beispiel
	for the very first time	zum allerersten Mal
	foreign	fremd
	forever	für immer
a	form	ein Formular
to	form	formen
	formal	förmlich, offiziell
a	fortune teller	eine Wahrsagerin, ein Wahrsager
	found	gefunden
	founded	gegründet
	fourteen	vierzehn
	free time	Freizeit
	freedom	Freiheit
to	freeze	gefrieren
	French	französisch
	French fries (AE)	Pommes Frites
a	friend	eine Freundin, ein Freund
	friendly, friendlier, the friendliest	freundlich, freundlicher, am freundlichsten
a	friendship	eine Freundschaft
	from	von, aus
	from all over the world	von überall her
in	front of	vor
	full of	voll mit, voll von
	fun	Spaß
	fur patterns	Fellmuster
	further	weitere, weiterer, weiteres
the	future	die Zukunft

G

to	gamble	um Geld spielen
a	game	ein Spiel
a	gap	eine Lücke
a	garage	eine Garage, eine Werkstatt
a	gardener	ein Gärtner, eine Gärtnerin
	garlic	Knoblauch
	gas (AE)	Benzin
a	gate	Flugsteig, Gate
	German	deutsch
a	gesture	eine Geste
to	get	bekommen
to	get sth.	etw. holen, etw. besorgen
to	get bored	sich langweilen
to	get dressed	sich anziehen
to	get to know someone	jemanden kennenlernen
to	get up	aufstehen
a	geysir	ein Geysir (Ort, wo heißes Wasser aus dem Boden spritzt)
a	girl	ein Mädchen
a	girlfriend	eine feste Freundin
to	give	geben
to	give out	herausgeben
	glad	froh
a	glove	ein Handschuh
to	go ahead	voran gehen, weitermachen
to	go camping	campen, zelten
to	go fishing	angeln gehen
to	go out	ausgehen (weggehen, zum Vergnügen)
to	go out with someone	mit jemandem (aus-)gehen
to	go shopping	einkaufen gehen
a	goal	ein Ziel

the	Gold Rush	der Goldrausch
a	goldfish	ein Goldfisch
	good, better	gut, guter/gute/ gutes
	Good luck.	Viel Glück.
a	good sense of humor	einen guten Humor
	goodbye	Auf Wiedersehen (Verabschiedung)
	Goodness!	Meine Güte!
	gothic	gotisch
a	graduate	eine Absolventin, ein Absolvent
to	graduate	absolvieren, die Schule erfolgreich beenden
a	graduation	die Schulab-schlussfeier
a	grandfather	ein Großvater
a	grandmother	eine Großmutter
	grandma	Oma
	grandpa	Opa
	grandparents	Großeltern
	great	großartig, toll
	Great Britain	Großbritannien
a	great-grandfather	ein Ur-Großvater
a	great-grandmother	eine Ur-Großmutter
	green	grün
a	greengrocer	ein/e Obst- und Gemüseverkäufer/in
a	greeting	eine Begrüßung
a	grid	ein Raster
	ground staff	Bodenpersonal (am Flughafen)
a	group	eine Gruppe
to	grow up	erwachsen werden

H

	hair	Haare
a	hair circlet	ein Haarreif
a	hair clasp	eine Haarspange
a	hair dryer	ein Fön
	hair gel	Haargel
	hair spray	Haarspray
a	hair tie	ein Haargummi
a	haircut	ein Haarschnitt
a	hairdresser	ein Frisör, eine Frisörin
a	hairstyle	Frisur
a	hand	eine Hand
to	hand	reichen
	hand baggage	Handgepäck
a	handbag	eine Handtasche
	handsome	gut aussehend
to	hang out	rumhängen, abhängen (ugs.)
to	hang out with some-one	mit jemandem rumhängen, abhängen (ugs.)
to	happen	passieren
	happy	glücklich
a	harbour	ein Hafen
	hard	hart, schwer, schwierig
a	hat	ein Hut
	hate	hassen
to	have	haben
to	have a look around	sich umschauen
to	have a look at	sich … anschauen
to	have breakfast	frühstücken
to	have butterflies in the stomach	Schmetterlinge im Bauch haben ➔ verliebt sein
to	have/take a shower	duschen
a	headband	ein Stirnband
a	heart	ein Herz
the	height	die Größe
	held	gefangen gehalten
a	helmet	ein Helm
to	help	helfen
	her	ihr, ihre
	here	hier
	Here you are.	Bitte schön (beim Überreichen von etwas.)

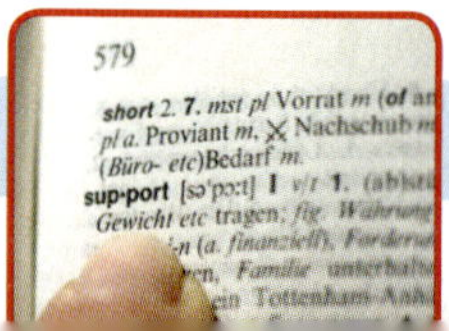

a	hero	ein Held
	herself	sich selbst (bei weiblichen Personen)
	hidden	versteckt
	hiking	wandern
	him	ihn, ihm
	himself	er selbst
a	hip	eine Hüfte
	his	sein, seine
a	histogram	ein Histogramm
	historical	historisch
	history	Geschichte
a	hit	ein Treffer
to	hit	treffen/schlagen
a	hobby (pl. hobbies)	ein Hobby (Hobbys)
	home	daheim
a	home	ein Zuhause
a	homepage	eine Homepage
a	hometown	eine Heimatstadt
	homework	Hausaufgaben
	hope	Hoffnung
to	hope	hoffen
	horrible	schrecklich
a	hospital	ein Krankenhaus
	hot	heiß
an	hour	eine Stunde
a	house	ein Haus
	how	wie
	humorous	humorvoll
to	hurry up	sich beeilen
a	husband	ein Ehemann

I

	I	ich
	I can't stand it.	Ich kann es nicht ausstehen.
	I owe you.	Du hast was gut bei mir!
	ice cream	Eis(creme)
	icehockey	Eishockey
an	icon	ein Symbol
	ICT	Informations- und Kommunikations-technologie (Schulfach)
an	idea	eine Idee
	if	wenn, falls, ob
to	ignore	ignorieren
an	imagination	eine Vorstellung
to	imagine	vorstellen, phantasieren
	immediately	sofort
	important	wichtig
	impossible	unmöglich
	impressive	eindrucksvoll
to	improve	verbessern
	in	in
	in former times	früher
	incorrect	nicht richtig, falsch
	independence	Unabhängigkeit
	independent	unabhängig
	India	Indien
	information	Information, Informationen
to	injure	körperlich verletzen
an	injury	eine körperliche Verletzung
	inline skating	Inline skaten
	innocence	Unschuld
	inside	drinnen
an	interest	ein Interesse
to	interest	sich interessieren
	interesting	interessant
the	internet	das Internet
an	internet browser	ein Programm zum Surfen im Internet
an	interview	ein Interview
to	introduce	vorstellen
to	invent	erfinden
to	invite	jemanden einladen

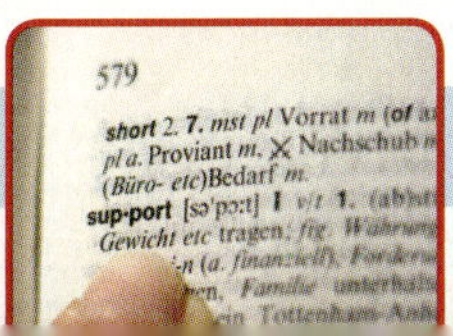

	It doesn't matter.	Es macht nichts.
	it's about ...	Es handelt sich um ...
an	item	ein Gegenstand

J

a	jacket	eine Jacke
	jeans	eine Jeans
	jewellery	Schmuck
	job	ein Job, eine Arbeit
a	job centre	ein Arbeitsamt
to	join	hinzukommen, sich beteiligen, verbinden, beitreten
a	journey	eine Reise
	judo	Judo
	July	Juli
a	jumper	ein Pullover
a	junction	eine Kreuzung
	just	nur, gerade eben

K

to	keep	behalten
to	keep fingers crossed	die Daumen drücken
to	keep in mind	bedenken
to	keep safe	sicher verwahren
a	keyboard	eine Tastatur
a	keyword	ein Schlüsselwort
	kids	Kinder
	killed	umgebracht
	Kind regards	Freundliche Grüße
	Kindest regards	Liebe Grüße
a	kiss	ein Kuss
to	kiss	küssen
to	know	wissen

L

to	label	beschriften
a, the	lady (pl. ladies)	eine Dame, die Damen
a	land	ein Land (geografisch)
a	language	eine Sprache
	large	groß
	Large	Kleidergröße **L**
	last	letzter, letzte, letztes
	late	spät
	later	später
	latest	neuestes
to	laugh	lachen
to	learn	lernen
to	leave	verlassen, lassen
a	leg	ein Bein
	leggings	Leggings
	legwarmers	Stulpen
	less	weniger
	let's	lass uns, lasst uns
a	letter	ein Brief, ein Buchstabe
a	letter of application	Bewerbungs-schreiben
	liberty	Freiheit
a	library	eine Bücherei
to	lie	liegen
a	life	ein Leben
the	lifestyle	der Lebensstil
a	lift	ein Fahrstuhl
	light (green)	hell (grün)
	lights	Lichter
	like	wie
to	like	mögen
the	likes	Dinge, die man mag
a	line chart	ein Linien-diagramm

a	lion	ein Löwe
a	lip	eine Lippe
a	lipstick	ein Lippenstift
a	list	eine Liste
a	list of pros and cons	eine Liste mit Für und Wider
to	listen to	anhören, zuhören
	listen to someone	jemandem zuhören
	little	klein, kleine, kleines
to	live	leben, wohnen
a	living room	ein Wohnzimmer
	local	am Ort
a	local market	örtlicher Markt/ Laden
	long	lang
a	look	ein Blick
to	look	schauen
to	look at	anschauen
to	look for	suchen
to	look forward to	sich auf etwas freuen
to	look like	aussehen wie
to	look up	nachschlagen
the	looks	das Aussehen
a	lorry	ein Lastwagen
a	lorry driver	ein LKW-Fahrer, eine LKW-Fahrerin
to	lose	verlieren
	lost	verloren
a	lot of fun	eine Menge Spaß
	lots of	viele
	loud, louder, the loudest	laut, lauter, am lautesten
to	love	lieben, gern mögen
a	love story	eine Liebes-geschichte
	lovely	lieblich
	lyrics	ein Liedtext

M

a	machine	eine Maschine
a	magazine	eine Zeitschrift
	mail	Post
to	make	machen
to	make good money	gutes Geld verdienen
to	make sure	sicherstellen
to	make yourself at home	sich heimisch fühlen
	make-up	Schminke
a	male	eine männliche Person
a	man (pl. men)	ein Mann
	many	viele
	March	März
to	mark	markieren
to	marry	heiraten
	mascara	Wimperntusche
a	match	Spiel, Match, etwas Zusammenpassen-des
to	match	zwei Menschen oder Dinge verbin-den, Paare finden, zusammenbringen, zuordnen
	matching	Verkupplung
a	matchmaker	ein Verkuppler, eine Verkupplerin
a	mausoleum	ein Grabmal
	may	können (Möglichkeit)
	May	Mai
	maybe	vielleicht
	me	mir, mich
to	mean	bedeuten
a	meaning	eine Bedeutung
	meantime	Zwischenzeit
a	mechanic	ein Mechaniker, eine Mechanikerin

	Medium	Kleidergröße **M**
to	meet	treffen
a	meeting	ein Treffen
a	meeting point	ein Treffpunkt
a	memorial	eine Gedenkstätte, ein Denkmal
a	men's department	eine Abteilung für Männerbekleidung
a	message	eine Nachricht
	might	könnten vielleicht
	mimic	Mimik
a	miniskirt	ein Minirock
a	minute	eine Minute
	… minutes are up.	… Minuten sind vorbei.
a	mirror	ein Spiegel
to	miss	verpassen, vermissen
	missing	fehlend
a	mistake	ein Fehler
to	mix	vermischen
a	mobile (phone)	ein Mobiltelefon, ein Handy
a	model	ein Model
a	mom, mum, momma	eine Mutter – Kosename (amerik. britisch)
	Monday	Montag
	(on) Mondays	montags
	money	Geld
a	monologue	ein Monolog
a	month	ein Monat
	moody	launisch
	more than	mehr als
a	morning	ein Morgen
(the)	most	am meisten
	most famous	am berühmtesten
	mostly	meistens, meist
a	mother	eine Mutter
a	mountain	ein Berg
a	mouse	eine Maus
to	move	ziehen, bewegen
a	movie (AE)	ein Film
a	movie-theatre (AE)	ein Kino
the	movies (AE)	das Kino
	much	viel
	multilingual	mehrsprachig
	music	Musik
a	must	ein Muss
	mutual	gegenseitig
	my	mein, meine

N

a	name	ein Name
to	name	benennen
	nasty	gemein, scheußlich, ekelhaft
a	national anthem	eine National-hymne
a	national holiday	ein Nationalfeiertag
a	national park	ein Nationalpark
a	Native American	ein Indianer, eine Indianerin
	necessary	nötig
a	necklace	eine Kette
to	need	brauchen, benötigen
a	neighbour	ein Nachbar, eine Nachbarin
	neon	Neon-
	nervous	nervös
	never	niemals, nie
	new	neu, neue, neues
a	newspaper	eine Zeitung
	next	nächster, nächste, nächstes
	next to	neben
	nice	nett, schön
a	nickname	ein Spitzname
a	night	eine Nacht
a	nightmare	ein Albtraum

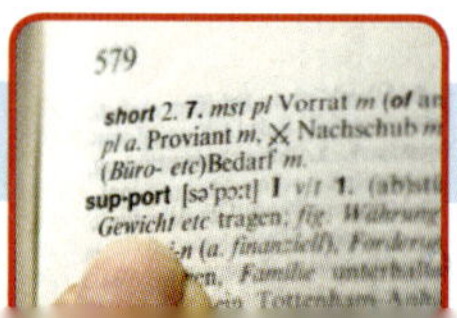

	no	nein, kein, keine, keines
	no more	nicht mehr
a	no-go	ein No-go, etw. ist unmöglich
	nobody	niemand
a	noise	ein Geräusch
	not	nicht
	not … anymore	nicht mehr
to	not care about	sich nicht viel daraus machen
	not yet	noch nicht
to	note	notieren, aufschreiben
	notes	Notizen
	now	jetzt
	nowadays	heutzutage
a	number	eine Nummer
to	number	nummerieren
a	nurse	eine Krankenschwester
to	nurse	pflegen
a	nursery teacher	ein Erzieher, eine Erzieherin

O

an	obligation	eine Verpflichtung
an	occasion	ein Anlass
	of course	natürlich
	off (I'm off at one o'clock.)	Ich habe um eins Schluss.
an	offer	ein Angebot
to	offer	anbieten
an	office	ein Büro
	often	oft
an	oil	ein Öl
to	oil	ölen
an	old people's home	ein Altersheim
	old, older, the oldest	alt, älter, am ältesten
	on	auf, an (bei elektronischen Geräten)
	on fire	brennen
	on sale	im Schlußverkauf
	oneself	man selbst
an	onion	eine Zwiebel
	online dating	online Verabreden
	only	nur
	open	offen
to	open	öffnen
an	opera	eine Oper
an	opinion	eine Meinung
	opposite	gegenüber
an	option	eine Alternative
	or	oder
an	order	eine Reihenfolge
to	order	bestimmen, anweisen
to	order sth.	etw. bestellen
to	organise	organisieren
an	organiser	ein Organisator, eine Organisatorin
	other	anderer, andere, anderes
	our	unser, unsere
	ourselves	uns selbst
	out	aus
	outside	draußen
	over	über
an	overall	ein Overall, ein Arbeitsanzug
to	overdo	übertreiben
	own	eigener, eigene, eigenes

P

a	page	eine Seite
a	pain	ein Schmerz
	painful	schmerzhaft
	paint	Farbe

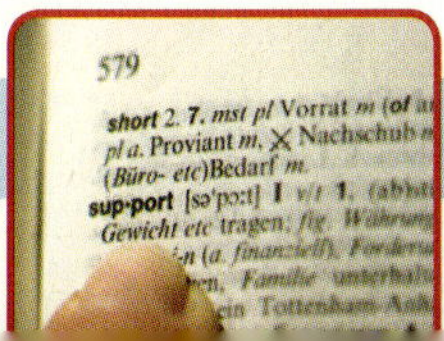

a	painter and decorator	ein Maler/Dekorateur, eine Malerin/Dekorateurin
a	pair	ein Paar
a	pair of jeans	eine Jeans
a	pal	Kumpel
a	palace	ein Palast
	pants (AE)	Hose
	paper	Papier
a	paperboy	ein Zeitungsausträger
a	papergirl	eine Zeitungsausträgerin
a	parade	eine Parade
	parents	Eltern
a	park	ein Park
to	park	parken
a	part	ein Teil
	particular	bestimmte, bestimmter, bestimmtes
a	partner	eine Partnerin, ein Partner
a	party	eine Party
a	passport	ein Reisepass
a	patch	ein Flicken
to	patch	flicken
a	patchwork	ein Flickwerk
a	pavement	ein Bürgersteig
to	pay	zahlen, bezahlen
	peace	Frieden
a	pedestrian precinct	eine Fußgängerzone
a	pencil	ein Bleistift
a	pencil skirt	ein Bleistiftrock
a	penny (pence)	ein Penny (Währung in GB)
	people	Leute, Menschen
a	permission	eine Erlaubnis
	per month	pro Monat
	perfect	perfekt
a	perfume	ein Parfüm

a	period	eine Phase, ein Abschnitt
	permanent wave	Dauerwelle
a	person	eine Person
a	pet	ein Haustier
	petrol	Benzin
a	petticoat	ein Petticoat, ein Unterrock
a	photo	ein Foto
a	photo album	ein Fotoalbum
a	photo(graph)	ein Foto
a	phrase	ein Satz, eine Redewendung
to	pick up	„anbaggern“, „anmachen“
a	pick-up line	ein Anmachspruch
a	picnic	ein Picknick
a	picture	ein Bild
to	picture	abbilden/beschreiben
a	piece	ein Stück
a	piece of paper	ein Stückchen Papier, ein Zettel
a	piston	ein Kolben (KFZ)
a	place	ein Ort, ein Platz, ein Sitz
a	plan	ein Plan
	platform shoes	Plateauschuhe
to	play	spielen
to	play cards	ein Kartenspiel spielen
	please	bitte
a	pleasure	ein Vergnügen
a	plumber	ein Klempner, eine Klempnerin
	p.m.	am Nachmittag, abends (bei Uhrzeiten)
a	pocket	eine Tasche
a	poem	ein Gedicht
the	Police (nur pl.)	die Polizei
	polite	höflich
	political	politisch

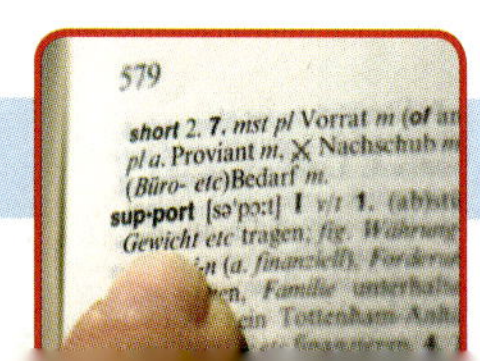

a	political map	eine Karte mit Ländergrenzen
	poor	arm
a	popstar	ein Popstar
	population	Bevölkerung
a	portrait	ein Portrait
a	possibility	eine Möglichkeit
the	possibilities	Möglichkeiten
a	postbox	ein Briefkasten
a	poster	ein Poster
a	pound	ein Pfund (Währung in GB)
	powder	Puder
to	prefer	bevorzugen
to	prefer sth.	etw. vorziehen, bevorzugen
to	prepare	vorbereiten
to	present	präsentieren, zeigen
a	presentation	eine Präsentation
a	president	ein Präsident
	pretty	hübsch
a	price	ein Preis (Geld)
a	price tag	ein Preisschild
a	prince	ein Prinz
a	princess	eine Prinzessin
	principles	Prinzipien
to	print	drucken
a	printer	ein Drucker
	privat	geheim, privat
a	prize	ein Preis (Gewinn)
	probable	wahrscheinlich
a	problem	ein Problem
	problematic	problematisch, schwierig
to	proceed	weitermachen
	productive	produktiv
a	profession	ein Beruf
a	profile	ein Profil
a	program	Programm
to	pronounce	aussprechen
	pros	Argumente für eine Sache
a	protection	ein Schutz
	proud	stolz
a	pub	eine Kneipe
	public holiday	(gesetzlicher) Feiertag
a	pullover	ein Pullover
	punctuation	Satzzeichen
a	purpose	ein Zweck, eine Absicht, ein Ziel
to	put something down	etwas hinlegen
to	put on	anziehen (Kleidung)
to	put some make-up on	sich schminken

Q

a	question	eine Frage
to	question	fragen, befragen
a	questionnaire	ein Fragebogen
	quick	schnell
a	quiz	ein Rätsel
a	quote	ein Zitat

R

a	radio station	ein Radiosender
to	raft	Wildwasser fahren
a	rainbow	ein Regenbogen
	rainy	regnerisch
	random	zufällig
a	razor	ein Rasierer
to	read	lesen, vorlesen
to	read along	mitlesen
	ready	fertig, bereit
	real	echt, real, wirklich
a	real life situation	eine echte Situation aus dem Leben
a	reason	ein Grund

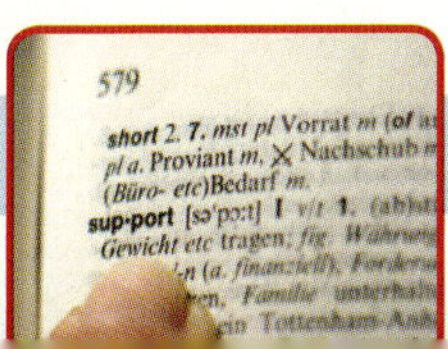

a	receiver	ein Empfänger, eine Empfängerin
	red	rot
a	relative	ein Verwandter, eine Verwandte
to	relax	entspannen, ausruhen
	reliable	zuverlässig, verlässlich
to	rely on someone	sich auf jemanden verlassen
to	remember	erinnern
a	rent	eine Miete
to	rent	mieten
a	rental contract	ein Mietvertrag
to	repair	reparieren
to	repeat	wiederholen
to	report	berichten
a	research	Recherche, Nachforschung
a	responsibility	eine Verantwortung
	responsible	verantwortlich
a	restaurant	ein Restaurant
a	result	ein Ergebnis, ein Resultat
a	retreat	ein Rückzug
to	retreat	sich zurückziehen
a	revival	ein Wiederer-wachen
to	rhyme	sich reimen
	rich	reich, reiche, reiches
a	ride	eine Fahrt
	right	richtig, rechts
a	right	ein Recht
	right now	jetzt, im Moment
a	ring	hier: ein Fingerring
to	ring	klingeln, läuten
a	river	ein Fluss
a	river bank	ein Flussufer
a	role	eine Rolle
a	roll	ein Würfelwurf
to	roll	rollen
	romantic	romantisch
a	roofer	ein Dachdecker, eine Dachdeckerin
a	room	ein Zimmer
a	round	eine Runde
a	row	eine Zeile
a	rubber	ein Radiergummi
a	rule	eine Regel
a	ruler	ein Lineal
to	run	rennen
to	run away	weglaufen
	running late	zu spät dran sein, zu spät kommen

S

	sad	traurig
	safe	sicher
a	salary	ein Gehalt
to	salute	salutieren
the	same	dieselbe, die gleiche
	satisfied	zufrieden
	Saturday	Samstag
to	save	retten, in Sicherheit bringen, speichern (PC)
to	save the world	die Welt retten
to	save time	Zeit sparen
to	say	sprechen, sagen
a	second	eine Sekunde
	scales	eine Waage
to	scan	etwas überfliegen, schnell lesen, scannen
a	scanner	ein Scanner
	scared	verängstigt
a	scarf	ein Schal, ein Halstuch
a	school	eine Schule
a	school report	ein Schulzeugnis
a	schoolyard	ein Schulhof

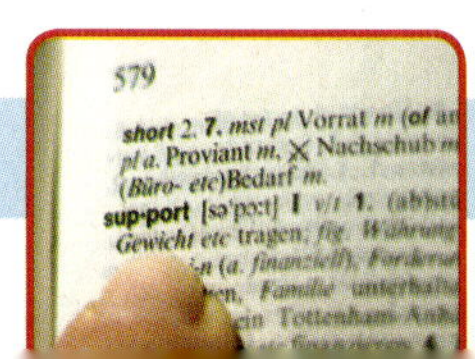

a	schoolmate	ein Schulkamerad, eine Schulkameradin
a	scooter	ein Scooter, ein Wagen
a	screen	ein Bildschirm
a	search	eine Suche
a	search engine	eine Suchmaschine
	second	zweiter, zweite, zweites
a	secret	ein Geheimnis
	security	Sicherheitskräfte
to	see	sehen, schauen
to	sell sth.	etw. verkaufen
to	send	senden, schicken
a	sense	ein Gespür
a	sentence	ein Satz
	service	Service
	several	mehrere
	shampoo	Shampoo
a	share	ein Anteil
to	share	teilen
to	shave	rasieren
	shaving foam	Rasierschaum
	shiny	glänzend
a	ship	ein Schiff
a	shirt	ein Hemd
a	shoe	ein Schuh
a	shop	ein Geschäft, ein Laden
a	shop assistant	ein Verkäufer, eine Verkäuferin
a	shop window	ein Schaufenster
a	shopping bag	eine Einkaufstasche
a	shopping centre	ein Einkaufszentrum
a	shopping tour	ein Einkaufsbummel
	short, shorter, the shortest	kurz, kürzer, am kürzesten
	should	sollten
	shoulderpads	Schulterpolster
to	show	zeigen
a	shower	eine Dusche
to	shower	duschen
	shower gel	Duschgel
	shy	schüchtern
a	sidewalk (AE)	ein Bürgersteig
a	sight	eine Sehenswürdigkeit
a	sign	ein Schild
to	sign	unterschreiben
	similar	ähnlich
	since	seit
to	sing	singen
a	single	ein Single (jemand ohne Partner/in), Einzel-
a	sink	ein Waschbecken
a	sister	eine Schwester
to	sit	sitzen
to	sit down	sich hinsetzen
a	situation	eine Situation
	sixteen	sechzehn
a	size	eine Größe
a	skill	eine Fähigkeit
a	skirt	ein Rock
a	skyline	die Silhouette einer Stadt
a	skyscraper	ein Wolkenkratzer
a	sleeve	ein Ärmel
	small, **S**mall	klein, auch: Kleidergröße **S**
	small talk	Smalltalk (oberflächliches Gespräch)
	smart	klug
a	smile	ein Lächeln
	sneakers	Turnschuhe
	snowy	es schneit
	so	so
	soap	Seife
	soccer (AE)	Fußball

a	social network	soziales Netzwerk (SchülerVZ, MySpace etc.)
a	software programmer	ein Programmierer, eine Programmie-rerin
a	soldier	ein Soldat, eine Soldatin
a	solution	eine Lösung
to	solve	lösen
	some	einige
	somebody	jemand
	someone	jemand
	something	etwas
	sometimes	manchmal
a	son	ein Sohn
a	song	ein Lied
	soon	bald
	sorry	Es tut mir Leid
a	soul	eine Seele
to	sound (It sounds like a plan.)	klingen, sich anhören (Das hört sich nach einem Plan an.)
	South Africa	Südafrika
	space	Weltraum
a	space ship	ein Raumschiff
to	speak	sprechen
	special	besonders
	spectacular	spektakulär
a	speech bubble	eine Sprechblase
	speed	Geschwindigkeit
a	speed dating	ein Treffen für Partnersuchende, bei dem sich jeder für eine kurze Zeit mit jedem unterhält
to	spell	buchstabieren
to	spend	verbringen, ausgeben
to	spend time	Zeit verbringen
	sports	Sport
	sports shoes	Sportschuhe
	sporty, sportier, the sportiest	sportlich, sportlicher, am sportlichsten
a	spot	ein Fleck, eine Stelle
	spring	Frühling
to	stand for	für … stehen
to	stand up	aufstehen
a	star	ein Stern, ein Star
	star-spangled	mit Sternen übersät
to	stare at	anstarren
to	start	starten, beginnen
a	state	ein Staat
the	Statue of Liberty	die Freiheitsstatue
a	stay	ein Aufenthalt
to	stay	bleiben
a	step	eine Stufe, ein Schritt
a	step-brother	ein Stiefbruder
a	stewardess	eine Flugbeglei-terin
	still	immer noch
a	stomach	ein Bauch
a	store	ein Laden
a	story	eine Geschichte
	straight (hair)	glatte (Haare)
a	strand of hair	eine Haarsträhne
a	stranger	ein Fremder, eine Fremde
a	strategy	eine Strategie
a	street	eine Straße
	stressful	stressig
a	stripe	ein Streifen
	striped	gestreift
	strong, stronger,the strongest	stark, stärker, am stärksten
	styling	das Styling
a	subject	ein Unterrichtsfach, ein Thema
to	subscribe	abonnieren
a	subscription	ein Abonnement
	such as	so wie, so etwas wie

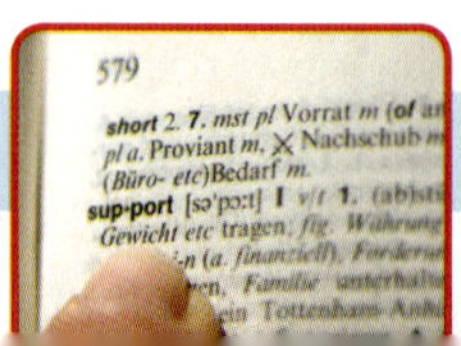

to	suit	passen
a	suitcase	ein Koffer
a	summer	ein Sommer
	sunglasses	eine Sonnenbrille
	sunny	sonnig
a	supermarket	ein Supermarkt
	sure	sicher
to	surf (on) the internet	im Internet surfen
a	surname	ein Nachname
a	surprise	eine Überraschung
a	survey	eine Erhebung, Umfrage
a	sweetheart	ein Liebling
	sweets	Süßigkeiten
to	swim	schwimmen
a	symbol	ein Symbol

T

a	T-shirt	ein T-Shirt
a	tab	ein Wasserhahn
a	table (e.g. in a kitchen)	ein Tisch
a	table (e.g. on a sheet of paper)	eine Tabelle
to	take	nehmen
to	take care of	sich um … kümmern
to	take dogs for a walk	Gassi gehen
to	take notes	Notizen aufschreiben
to	take time for sth.	sich Zeit nehmen
a	talk	ein Gespräch
to	talk	sprechen, reden
	talkative	gesprächig
	tall, taller, the tallest	groß, größer, am größten
a	taxi (AE)	ein Taxi
a	taxi driver	ein Taxifahrer, eine Taxifahrerin
a	taxi stand	ein Taxistand
a	teacher	eine Lehrerin, ein Lehrer
	technology	Technologie
a	telephone	ein Telefon
a	telephone number	eine Telefonnummer
a	telephone receiver	ein Telefonhörer
a	television	ein Fernseher
to	tell	erzählen
	tender	zart, weich
	tennis	Tennis
a	text	ein Text
a	textbook	ein Lesebuch
	than	als
to	thank someone	sich bei jemandem danken
	that	dass
	the	der, die, das
a	theatre	ein Theater
	their	ihr, ihre (Plural)
	them	sie, ihnen
	themselves	sich/ihnen selbst
	then	dann
	there	dort, da, dahin
	they	sie (Plural)
a	thing	ein Ding
to	think	denken
to	think of something or someone	an etwas oder jemanden denken
	this way	hier entlang, auf diese Weise
	those	diese
	though	obwohl, dennoch
	three	drei
	through	durch
	thundering	donnernd
	Thursday	Donnerstag
	(on) Thursdays	donnerstags
to	tick	einen Haken machen, abhaken
a	ticket	ein Ticket (Flugschein)

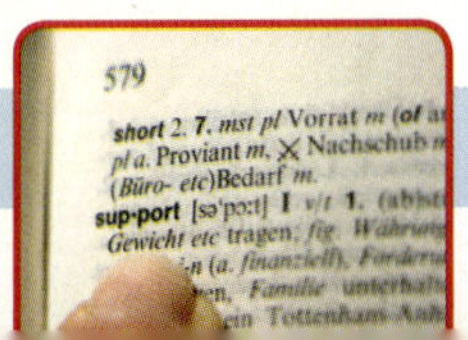

	ticket sale	Ticketverkaufs-schalter
	tights	eine Strumpfhose
	time	Zeit
a	tire	ein Reifen
a	title	ein Titel, eine Überschrift
	to	zu, an
	today	heute
a	token	ein Spielstein
	tomorrow	morgen
	tonight	heute Nacht
	too	auch
	too (big)	zu (groß)
a	tool	ein Werkzeug
a, the	tooth (pl. teeth)	ein Zahn, die Zähne
a	toothbrush	eine Zahnbürste
a	toothpaste	eine Zahnpasta
a	top	ein Oberteil, ein Top
a	topic	ein Thema
	totally	total
to	touch	berühren
a	town	eine Stadt
a	Town Hall, City Hall	ein Rathaus
a	toy	ein Spielzeug
	trades of character	Charakterzüge
	traffic	Straßenverkehr
	traffic lights	(eine) Ampel
a	transfer	eine Übertragung
to	transfer	übertragen
to	translate	übersetzen
a	translation	eine Übersetzung
to	travel	reisen
a	tree	ein Baum
	trendy	modisch, schick
a	trip	ein Ausflug
	trouble	Ärger
	(pair of) trousers	Hose
a	truck (AE)	ein Lastwagen
	true	wahr
a	trunk (AE)	ein Kofferraum
to	trust	vertrauen
to	try	probieren
	Tuesday	Dienstag
to	turn	wenden
a	turn (It's your turn.)	ein Spielzug (Du bist am Zug.)
to	turn over	umdrehen
a	TV	ein Fernseher
a	two-year-old son	ein zweijähriger Sohn
to	type	tippen
	typical	typisch

U

	ugly	hässlich
	ultimately	letztendlich
an	umbrella	ein Regenschirm
	unattended	unbeaufsichtigt
an	uncle	ein Onkel
	uncomfortable	unbehaglich, verlegen
	under	unter
	unfriendly	unfreundlich
	unhealthy	ungesund
the	United States of America	die Vereinig-ten Staaten von Amerika
	until	bis
	unusual	nicht normal, ungewöhnlich
	us	uns
to	use	benutzen, verwenden
	useful	nützlich
	usual	normal, gewöhnlich
	usually	normalerweise, eigentlich

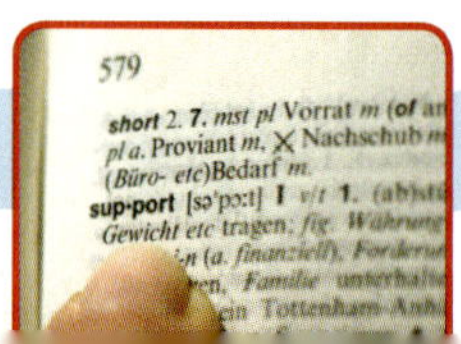

V

	vacation	Ferien
a	vehicle	ein Fahrzeug
	very	sehr
	Vietnam	Vietnam
a	village	ein Dorf
a	virus	ein (Computer) Virus
to	visit	besuchen
	voluntary work	freiwillige Arbeit
to	volunteer	sich freiwillig melden

W

to	wait	warten
a	waiting area	ein Warteraum
a	waitress, waiter	eine Kellnerin, ein Kellner
to	wake up	aufwachen
a	walk	ein Spaziergang
a	wall	eine Wand
to	want	wollen
a	war	ein Krieg
	was	war
to	wash	waschen
a	watch	eine Armbanduhr
to	watch	ansehen
a	waterfall	ein Wasserfall
to	wave	wehen
a	way	ein Weg
	we	wir
to	wear	tragen
the	weather	das Wetter
a	weather forecast	ein Wetterbericht
a	website	eine Internetseite
	Wednesday	Mittwoch
a	week	eine Woche
a	weekend	ein Wochenende
to	welcome	Willkommen heißen
	well	also
	what	was
	What would I do without you?	Was würde ich ohne dich tun?
	What's the matter?	Was ist los?
	What's up?	Was ist los? Was läuft?
	What's going on?	Was ist los?
	whatever	was auch immer
	when	wann, wenn, als
	where	wo
	where else	Wo noch?
	which	welcher, welche, welches
	while	während
	white	weiß
	who	wer
	who knows	wer weiß
	whole	ganz, ganze, ganzer, ganzes
	whom	wem
	whose	wessen, dessen
	why	warum
	wide	breit
a	wife (pl. wives)	eine Ehefrau (Ehefrauen)
	wild	wild
	will	wollen, etwas tun werden
to	win	gewinnen
a	window seat	Fensterplatz
	windy	windig
a	winner	ein Gewinner, eine Gewinnerin
a	winter	ein Winter
	with	mit, bei
	without	ohne
a	witness	eine Zeugin, ein Zeuge
to	witness	bezeugen
a	wooly hat	eine Wollmütze
a	woman (pl. women)	eine Frau, Frauen
to	wonder	sich fragen

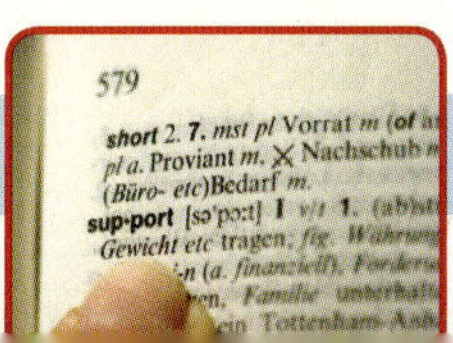

	wonderful	wunderbar
a	word	ein Wort
a	work	eine Arbeit
to	work	arbeiten
a	work experience	ein Praktikum
a	workbook	ein Arbeitsheft
the	working boots	die Arbeitsschuhe
the	working clothes	die Arbeitskleidung
the	working hours	die Arbeitszeit
the	working trousers	die Arbeitshose
	worried	besorgt
	would	würden
to	wrest	entreißen, gewaltsam wegnehmen
to	write	schreiben
to	write down	aufschreiben
	wrong	falsch

X

a	x-axis	eine x-Achse

Y

a	y-axis	eine y-Achse
a	year	ein Jahr
a	yell	brüllender Schrei
to	yell	brüllen
the	Yellow pages	Die Gelben Seiten (Telefonbuch)
	yes	ja
	you	du, ihr
	You will look stunning!	Du wirst atemberaubend/umwerfend aussehen!
	young, younger, the youngest	jung, jünger, am jüngsten
	your	dein, deine, euer, eure
	Yours	Abschiedsgruß: Dein/Deine
	Yours faithfully	Mit freundlichen Grüßen
	Yours sincerely	Mit freundlichen Grüßen
	yourself	du selbst, dir selbst, euch selbst
a	youth club	ein Jugendtreff
a	youth hostel	eine Jugendherberge

Z

a	zebra	ein Zebra
a	zoo	ein Zoo

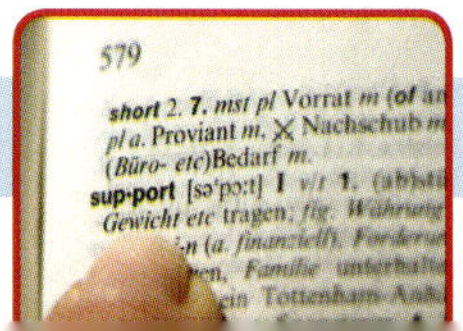

Beginn und Ende	
Good morning. How are you?	Guten Morgen. Wie geht es dir/euch/Ihnen?
Good bye. See you tomorrow.	Auf Wiedersehen. Bis morgen.
Fragen	
Can you help me?	Kannst du mir/Können Sie mir helfen?
What's "Freunde treffen" in English?	Was heißt „Freunde treffen“ auf Englisch?
What's "meeting friends" in German?	Was heißt „meeting friends“ auf Deutsch?
Could you say that again?	Kannst du/Können Sie das wiederholen?
Can I borrow your ruler?	Kann ich mir dein/Ihr Lineal ausleihen?
Can I go to the toilet?	Darf ich zur Toilette gehen?
Arbeitsanweisungen	
Listen to the CD, please.	Höre dir/Hört euch die CD an.
Match the words and the pictures.	Ordne/ordnet die Wörter den Bildern zu.
You need a pencil/ruler.	Du/Ihr braucht einen Bleistift/ein Lineal.
Hold an interview.	Führe/Führt ein Interview durch.
Let's make a list.	Lasst uns eine Liste machen.
Open your books on page …, please.	Schlagt bitte eure Bücher auf Seite ... auf.
Work with a partner.	Arbeitet mit einem Partner.
Work in teams of four.	Arbeitet zu viert.
Write down your answers.	Schreibt eure Antworten auf.
Act the scene.	Spiele/Spielt es vor.
Come to the board, please.	Komme bitte an die Tafel.
Come and sit in a circle.	Kommt her und macht einen Sitzkreis.

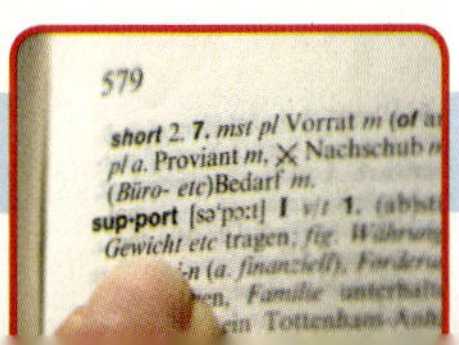

Lob, Ermahnung und Dank	
That's right. Very good. Well done.	Das ist richtig. Sehr gut. Gut gemacht.
Attention, please. Listen to me.	Ich bitte um Aufmerksamkeit. Hört mir zu.
Be quiet, please.	Bitte seid leise.
Thank you. Thank you very much.	Danke. Vielen Dank.
Entschuldigung	
Sorry, I'm late.	Entschuldigen Sie die Verspätung.
Sorry, I don't have my book/my homework/my pencil.	Entschuldigung, ich habe mein Buch/meine Hausaufgaben/meinen Bleistift nicht.

Bildquellenverzeichnis

© Childnet International - www.childnet.com: S. 14

© dpa picture-alliance GmbH, Frankfurt: S. 22 r. M., 24 zweites v. o. l. (chromorange), 45 o., 49, 69, 79, 87 o., 102 o., 113 o.

© Fotolia, New York: S. 10 (Jerome Dancette, liam17, Rudolf Tepfenhart, AHMAD FAIZAL YAHYA), 11 (Marcus Kästner, Dreef, lassedesignen, Klaus-Peter Adler), 12 (iofoto, Julián Rovagnati, Earl Robbins, Klaus-Peter Adler, Smileus, Mademoiselle Bézier, deanm1974, AHMAD FAIZAL YAHYA, Ewe Degiampietro, 15 o. (stiven), 15 u. (Toby Lord), 22 (l. o.: Roman Millert, r. o.: by-studio, l. M.: SergeylT, Mario Matos, l. u.: Concept web Studio, r. u.: Liv Friis-larsen), 24 (Ferenc Szelepcsenyi, chestra, Kaarsten, Franz Pfluegl, Donald Joski, Nikolay Okhitin, gem), 26 (Michael Flippo), 27 (by-studio), 28/29 (Franz Pfluegl, Frank Eckgold, Monkey Business, Patrizia Tilly, Antonio Nunes, Galina Barskaya, puje, Amir Kaljikovic, mars), 32 o. (PicturenetCorp), 32 M. (klickit), 32 u., 33 (Studio-54, CURAphotography, Andres Rodriguez, TheSupe87), 37 o. (babsi_w), 37 u. (pressmaster), 39 (moonrun), 46 (Vadim Ponomarenko, Alexander Yakovlev, Guido Thomasi, Jane Doe, Andreas Gradin, AndersonRise), 49 (Valna Vitaly, Amir Kaljikovic, Dmitri MIkitenko, Birgit Reitz-Hofmann, Gordan Gledec, Jennifer Stone), 50/51 (Gina Sanders, CatonPhoto, Szasz-Fabian Erika, aris sanjaya, Floris70, mangostock, Greg Pickens), 53 (Peter Atkins), 54 (Bobby Earle, Phototom, Amir Kaljikovic, AVAVA), 55 (Tasosk, jcarvalhozz, Andree Wendel, Thomas Durst, Bergfee, virtua73), 56 (photobunny), 57 (contrastwerkstatt, Floris70, CandyBoxPhoto, Dan Race, Monkey Business, EastWest Imaging), 60 (Monika Adamczyk, fotofrank, Floris70), 61 (CatonPhoto, CandyBoxPhoto, Szasz-Fabian Erika, Rade Lukovic, Rebecca Capell), 62/63 (Monkey Business, amelie, Konstantin Sutyagin, fafoutis, Klaus-Peter Adler, Franz Pfluegl, Akhilesh Sharma, 2GreenEyes, ExQuisine), 70 u. (Rena Marijn), 82/83 (kerstinR, Niklas Kratzsch, Marcus Kästner, Dendron, Konstantin Sutyagin, S Hagebusch, Winston Lue), 84 o. r.(kerstinR), 85 (Marcus Kästner, Dendron, Winston Lue), 86 (Niklas Kratzsch, Konstantin Sutyagin), 87 M. (Kevin Knuth), 87 u. (OutdoorPhoto), 88 (Andrew Tobin), 89 (adamgolabek, Peter), 90 (Ian O'Hanlon, Marc Dietrich), 94/95 (John Keith, buckwheat, Paige Roberts, Sandor Jackal, razihusin, Peter Baxter), 99 (Cheryl Casey, v0v, Carla Van Wagoner, RoJo Images), 102 (Peter), 103 (Sandor Jackal, Lisa F. Young, Monika Wisniewska, Feng Yu (2x), Paige Roberts, RoJo Images), 104/105 (Lisa F. Young, Digitalpress, Lim Jerry, Ilan Amith, Michael Homann, Glenda Powers, Kablonk Micro, Michael), 107 (R.Scheiwiller), 110 o. (Michael Homann), 110 u. (Ilan Amith), 112 (3x), 113 u. (Ferenc Szelepcsenyi), 128 l. (Gabriel Blaj), 128 r. (Daniel Terence Mock)

© getty images: Cover, S. 94 l. o., 95 r. o., 103 o. M.

© google: S. 98

© Hendrik Kranenberg/Bildungsverlag EINS: S. 6/7, 8, 13, 16/17, 18, 19, 20, 21, 23, 25, 26, 30, 31, 32, 34/35, 36, 40/41, 42, 43, 48, 52, 53, 59, 64, 65, 66, 67, 68, 70, 71, 72/73, 74, 75, 76, 77, 78, 80, 81 u., 88, 89, 91, 92, 93, 96, 97, 101, 106, 107, 109, 110, 111, 112, , 114/115, 124, 125, 128

© Marlene Pohle/BV1: S. 81 o.

© Martin Plewa – www.fotografx.org: S. 47

© MEV Verlag Gmbh, Augsburg: S. 28 r. M., 50 l. M., 50 r. M., 51 l. u., 51 r. u., 54 r. o., 54 r. u., 60 o., 60 u. l., 62 r. M., 82 l. o., 83 r. o., 84 o. l., 84 u.

© Microsoft Corperation: S. 9 (Screenshots)

© Project Photos: S. 24 viertes o.l.

© ullstein bild: S. 44 (3x), 45 u., 49, 82 l. u., 100 (2x), 101, 108

Textquellenverzeichnis

© Alecia B. Moore/Scott Spencer Storch: Family Portrait. EMI April Music Inc./TVT Music Inc., EMI Music Publishing (Germany GmbH), Hamburg

© John Lennon/Paul McCartney: Help. Northern Songs Ltd. Maclen Joint Ltd., Sony/ATV Music Publishing (Germany GmbH), Berlin

© Jay Livingston/Ray Evans: Qué sera – When I was just a little boy. 1985 by J. Livingston and St. Angelo Music L.A., D/A/CH: Melodie der Welt J Michel KG, Frankfurt, Neue Welt Musikverlag GmbH, München

© Micheal O. Bruce/Glen Buxton/Dennis Dunaway/Vincent Furnier/Neal A. Smith: School's out. EZRA MUSIC CORP/SIX PALMS MUSIC CORP., Melodie der Welt J. Michel KG Musikverlag, Frankfurt/M.